Caroline

Pop the Question

- Crosswords
- Cartoons
- Quizzes for all ages
- Word games
- Photoquiz
- Anagrams
- Hours of fun for the whole family

A message from
JOHNNIE WALKER

A radio quiz-game, now a book and it's all thanks to B.B.C. telephone balancing unit number PA8/351/113, which makes Pop the Question possible.

It's an impressive-looking gadget the Beeb technicians put together enabling a standard telephone to effectively function both as a receiver and a microphone, broadcasting to millions whatever is said by either of our contestants. So, freed from holding a telephone to each ear *and* wearing a pair of head-phones, I could now accept what has proved to be the most stimulating and challenging role in radio since becoming a D.J. in 1965.

My earlier experience as a salesman faced with total strangers in a car showroom has no doubt been of help in chairing Pop the Question, though of course at that time there wasn't a Radio One audience eavesdropping on the conversation.

There's a widely-held misconception that some Radio One programmes are recorded, or that there is a kind of 'delay' system at work on phone calls.

Not so.

Our trusty friend the balancing unit broadcasts live whatever happens to come down the line.

Like the guy who reacted to a question with a long pause and then, oh so drily, asked 'Can I call you back on that one John?' Much falling about in the studio following that.

There was the contestant struggling to recall the artist responsible for a certain hit record who said, 'Can't think who it was, and I've got the bloody record in my collection.'

And there was the classic that people still come up and ask me about. The young girl whose disappointment on losing proved just too much – she burst into tears and wailed 'I don't want a single (the consolation prize) I want an album.' Talking my way out of that situation was definitely not one of my easier moments.

But it is of course the unexpected happenings that go to make up the challenge I mentioned earlier. It's one I enjoy immensely and I hope to be in the Pop the Question 'hot-seat' for many more games to come.

I am, of course, just the front-man and it's nice to have the opportunity to give credit and thanks to people like David Rider, a bespectacled genius with the unenviable task of providing a constant flow of new questions. To executive producer Doreen Davies and Derek Chinnery, head of Radio One, for thinking up the original idea. My thanks to producers Roger Pusey and now Ron Belchier for their sterling work in dialling all the numbers and soothing nervous contestants. Thanks to 'the wives of the stars' who were brave enough to pose in front of an amateur's camera lens and to John Stanley for talking them into it.

The biggest bouquet of thanks goes of course to you the listener for making Pop the Question a success. With this book you can now be chairman as well as contestant. May the arguments be scarce and the fun plentiful.

23rd January 1975

JOHNNIE WALKER'S
Pop the Question

Compiled by David Rider

with cartoons by Trevor Chrismas

EVEREST BOOKS LTD
4 Valentine Place, London SE1

Published in Great Britain by Everest Books Ltd, 1975

A paperback original

ISBN 0903925 338

Copyright © 1975 by arrangement with the
British Broadcasting Corporation

This book is sold subject to the condition
that it shall not, by way of trade or
otherwise, be lent, re-sold, hired out or
otherwise circulated without the publisher's
prior consent in any form of binding or
cover other than that in which it is
published and without a similar condition
including this condition being imposed on the
subsequent purchaser.

Made and printed in Great Britain by
Hunt Barnard Printing Limited, Aylesbury, Bucks.

FOREWORD

The Head of Radio One, Derek Chinnery, and I were looking for an idea to replace the popular Astrology feature on 'The Johnnie Walker Show'.

We settled on a short daily pop quiz, and Johnnie's wife Frances, came up with the bright idea for the title, 'Pop the Question'.

The quiz was launched in May, 1972, and for the first year, another top Radio One D.J. Noel Edmonds, set the questions, but pressure of work compelled him to relinquish this task, and David Rider, an ex-B.B.C. Studio Manager, has been doing it ever since. So, as you can see, this has been one of those rare occasions when too many cooks didn't spoil the broth!

Everyone enjoys pitting their wits against each other, and it's this interesting facet of human nature, combined with Johnnie's obvious pleasure when talking to the participants, that has made this spot so successful. He always feels sorry for the unlucky contestants, but realises that everybody can't be a winner. However, with this book, *you* can know all the answers. So, at your next party, just see if you don't get instant attention as your guests try and outdo each other with their pop knowledge!

Doreen Davies
Executive Producer
Radio I

AUTHOR'S NOTE

Those of you who have listened to Pop the Question on Radio 1, or perhaps even taken part, will find that this book, whilst retaining certain features of the radio quiz, includes many things which cannot be done on the air. Obviously, our picture quizzes are a case in point but there are also word games and a crossword to break up the batches of ordinary questions of which there are some 600 for you to answer. So that all members of the family can take part, the range of questions has been extended to include the music and films of the 1930s and 1940s; but the bulk of them refer to music which has been popular in the 1950s, 1960s and 1970s. With a few exceptions, the Top Twenty forms the basis for the questions in which clues are quite often given to point you towards the right answer. Our telephone contestants do not realise, perhaps, that the questions which they have to answer are carefully phrased to make sure that they are not misled into giving a wrong answer. This is why constant reference is made to dates throughout the book, particularly as songs and records are often revived some years after their original success. Parts of this book have nearly driven me round the bend: I can only hope that they do the same for you!

David Rider
Sheffield Park
Sussex

POP THE QUESTION is divided into 12 rounds.

Every round includes five quizzes, each for a different age group: Weenyboppers (under 12); Teenyboppers (12–18); Teen-and-Twenties (18–30); Mums and Dads (30–45); and Grandparents (over 45).

Each round also features cartoons and a selection of novel puzzles.

The idea is for all ages to take part in a family competition.

The questions get harder as you progress through the book. Good luck!

ROUND 1: DEAD EASY

Weeny boppers

1. Complete this song title: ALRIGHT ALRIGHT . . . ?

2. Which group had hits with SHANG-A-LANG and SUMMERLOVE SENSATION?

3. Who lived in a YELLOW SUBMARINE?

4. Who sang about MY DING-A-LING?

5. What was the Chelsea Football Team's hit called?

6. Which American hit-maker starred in the television series called THE PARTRIDGE FAMILY?

7. Is country and western a kind of soup, a type of music or a bus company?

8. Which group had a hit with TIE A YELLOW RIBBON?

9. Who was KUNG FU FIGHTING in 1974?

10. Who said I'M THE LEADER OF THE GANG (I AM!)?

Teeny boppers

1. Dana had a No. 1 hit in 1970: what was her song called?

2. Did Mott the Hoople sing about ALL THE YOUNG NUDES, ALL THE YOUNG DUDES or ALL THE YOUNG PRUDES?

3. What sort of pie did Don McLean sing about? *American*

4. Who found herself in a ROSE GARDEN in 1971?

5. Who had a hit in 1974 with (YOU'RE) HAVING MY BABY? *Paul Anka.*

6. The England Football Squad were No. 1 in May 1970: what song did they sing?

7. Freda Payne had a big hit in 1970: what was it called?

8. Which group consists of Eric Faulkner, Alan Longmuir, Leslie McKeown, Derek Longmuir and Stuart Wood?

9. Complete this group's name: Blood, Sweat and ... ? *Tears*

10. Who praised the virtues of a MELTING POT in 1970? *Blue Mink*

Teen-and-Twenties

1. Who took YESTERDAY MAN and TO WHOM IT CONCERNS into the charts in 1965?

2. Some years ago the Beatles started their own record label: what did they call it? *Apple*

3. Who enjoyed chart success with SUGAR SUGAR in 1969? *Archers*

4. Correct this statement: BIG MOON RISING was a hit for Creedence Clearwater Reversal. *Revival*

5. Which American group had GOOD VIBRATIONS? *Beach Boys*

6. Who was the first disc jockey to broadcast on Radio 1?

7. Which band scored a big success with MR TAMBOURINE MAN in 1965? *Byrds*

8. With whom do you associate the hits GLAD ALL OVER and BITS AND PIECES?

9. Cliff Richard has represented Great Britain twice in the Eurovision Song Contest; what song did he sing the first time? *Congratulations*

10. Which British group had hits with BEND IT, OKAY and ZABADAK?

Mums and Dads

1. Which group had their first hit in 1964 with THE HOUSE OF THE RISING SUN? *Animals*

2. Which tune took German orchestra leader Helmut Zacharias into our Top 20 in 1964?

3. Which American jazzman had a hit with HELLO DOLLY in 1964?

4. Which is right: BUDDY HOLLY by Bo Diddley or BO DIDDLEY by Buddy Holly?

5. Who asked TAKE THESE CHAINS FROM MY HEART in 1963?

6. Which singer was most closely associated with the Twist? *Chubby Checker*

7. Which rock 'n' roll star, now dead, sang SUMMERTIME BLUES, C'MON EVERYBODY and THREE STEPS TO HEAVEN? *Eddie Cochran*

8. Which girl group had hits with THEN HE KISSED ME and DA DOO RON RON? *Crystals*

9. Who played SIDESADDLE and then tried a little ROULETTE?

10. What was the name of Billy J. Kramer's backing group?

Grandparents

1. Which singer, born in Rochdale, made her home on the Isle of Capri?

2. With which instrument do you associate Benny Goodman?

3. Who sang GOODNIGHT VIENNA in the film of that name?

4. With which British band did Dennis Lotis, Lita Roza and Dickie Valentine use to sing?

5. Who used to start his radio shows by shouting 'Wakey wakey!'?

6. Who wrote the song MAD DOGS AND ENGLISHMEN?

7. Which duo sang UNDERNEATH THE ARCHES, RUN RABBIT RUN and HOME TOWN?

8. Who made the song WHEN I'M CLEANING WINDOWS popular in 1937? *George Farmar*

9. Where did a nightingale sing?

10. Who is known as the Old Groaner? *F. Sinatra*

Four pop groups are represented here. Can you name them?

4 Tops

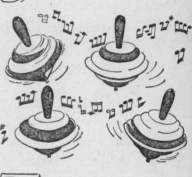

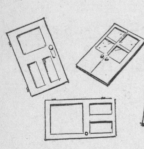
Doors

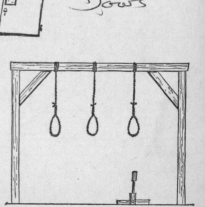

Stranglers

Who am I?

Each line in this puzzle gives you one letter and, when you have correctly deciphered the letters, they will give you the name of a popular girl singer.

My first is in CAME but not in CAPE   M

My second is in BARN but not in BURN   A

My third is in CARE but not in CAVE   V

My fourth is in RICE but not in RACE   I

My fifth is in FARE but not in FARM   E

My sixth is in BOAR but not in BEAR   O

My seventh is in SINE but not in FINE   S

My eighth is in RAMP but not in RASP   M

My ninth is in BORE but not in BARE   O

My tenth is in NICE but not in RICE   N

My last is in RAID but not in RAIN   D

Anagrams

Here are some simple anagrams to test your ingenuity. If you re-arrange each of these odd phrases you will get either the name of a group, a singer, a disc jockey or the title of a song. To help you, each answer in this section consists of only two words.

1. STAB THE LEE

2. AVID DISC DAYS

3. MY VEIL IS JAM

4. TRAM SALE GEM

5. BABY RULER

6. WEDS TREAT

7. DAD DIGS MOON

8. THEM BE SLOW

9. JOLT ON HEN

10. MY DONS DO NON

ROUND 2: EASY

Weeny boppers

1. Who told the story of ERNIE – THE FASTEST MILK-MAN IN THE WEST?

2. What is the name of the radio programme introduced by Ed Stewart on Radio 1 each Saturday and Sunday?

3. Lena Zavaroni had a big hit with her first single: what song did she sing?

4. Which British group had hits with CRAZY, HYPNOSIS and DYNAMITE?

5. What was Alvin Stardust's first hit called?

6. Which group had a hit with YOU WON'T FIND AN-OTHER FOOL LIKE ME?

7. Who had hits with PUPPY LOVE, WHY and TOO YOUNG?

8. Which American group, stars of a popular TV series, had hits with BREAKING UP IS HARD TO DO and LOOKIN' THROUGH THE EYES OF LOVE?

9. Who had a hit with PEPPER BOX in 1974?

10. Which duo had hits with WELCOME HOME, DON'T STAY AWAY TOO LONG and RAINBOW?

Teeny boppers

1. Which American act had hits with TOP OF THE WORLD and CLOSE TO YOU? *Carpenters*

2. SON OF MY FATHER was a No. 1 hit in 1972: who for? *Chicory Tip*

3. Was YELLOW RIVER a hit for Mungo Jerry, Christie or Butterscotch?

4. According to the Faces, was Cindy accidentally or <u>incidentally?</u>

5. Who shot to No. 1 in 1971 with DOUBLE BARREL?

6. Andy Scott, Steve Priest and Mick Tucker are three of the Sweet: who's the fourth? *Billy Connolly.*

7. Who went on a SEASIDE SHUFFLE in 1972? *Terry Dactal & the Dinarsaurs*

8. What is the name of the Who's lead singer? *R Daltrey*

9. Which lady did Cat Stevens serenade in 1970? *Lady D'arbanville*

10. I AM I SAID he sang, and then had a SONG SUNG BLUE: who is he?

   Neil Diamond

Teen-and-Twenties

1. Who had a hit with SPANISH FLEA in 1966?

2. Who went to a SHOTGUN WEDDING?

3. Who sang about a BOY NAMED SUE in 1969? *Jonny Cash*

4. Who took WITH A LITTLE HELP FROM MY FRIENDS to No. 1 in 1968?

5. What kind of bird did the Plastic Ono Band sing about in 1969? *Cold Turkey.*

6. Who rode on the MARRAKESH EXPRESS?

7. Who had a hit in 1969 with the curiously titled IT MEK?

8. What instrument is played by hit-maker Duane Eddy? *Guitar*

9. In 1967, Vince Hill had a hit with a song from a famous stage and screen musical: what was the song called?

10. ELP is the abbreviated name of which group?
    Emerson/Lake/Palmer

Mums and Dads

1. THINGS, MULTIPLICATION and MACK THE KNIFE: who had hits with these songs?

2. What song did Susan Maughan take into the Top 10 in 1962?

3. YEH YEH was a No. 1 hit in 1964: who for?

4. Which group said YOU'VE GOT YOUR TROUBLES in 1965?

5. Who had a VACATION in 1962?

6. Who used to introduce the long running radio show PICK OF THE POPS?

7. Who invited you to ROCK AROUND THE CLOCK in 1955?

8. What was the title of the Honeycombs' first hit in 1964?

9. Lord Rockingham's XI had a hit with a Scottish sounding title in 1958: what was it called?

10. Who was chairman of the popular TV programme JUKE BOX JURY?

Grandparents

1. Who wrote the music for the hit shows THE DANCING YEARS and KING'S RHAPSODY?

2. Who wanted you to sail ON THE GOOD SHIP LOLLI-POP? *Shirley Temple*

3. Who was once PUTTIN' ON THE STYLE and said DON'T YOU ROCK ME DADDY-O?

4. Which American singer was known as the Nabob of Sob?

5. Today, enthusiastic young girl fans are called teeny-boppers: what were they called in the 1940s?

6. Who was Fred Astaire's most famous dancing partner? *Ginger Rogers*

7. Which record label has a £ sign as its trade mark? *Parlophone*

8. Which popular band leader used SAY IT WITH MUSIC as his theme tune?

9. With which vocal group do you associate the song WHISPERING GRASS?

10. What instrument did Eddy Duchin play?

Name the two Tamla-Motown hits illustrated here.

My Guy

Rockin' Robin

Quizzigram

First of all, solve the clues which are given below and put the words into the diagram with the first letter of each word in the left-hand column. When the letters in this column are rearranged they give the name of a popular American singer.

1. Twelve months (4)
2. A cold country (7)
3. Alvin's surname (8)
4. The Top Twenty (5)
5. Rupie Edwards had these feelings (3)
6. An Osmond christian name (4)
7. A record (4)
8. Calf meat (4)
9. Comic Ken (4)
10. Collection of soldiers (4)
11. It rises and sets every day (3)
12. Miss Springfield's christian name (5)

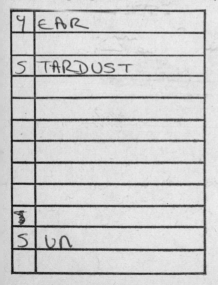

Lyrics

Here are ten extracts from some popular songs. Can you say what the title of the song is in each case and who made it into a hit?

1. 'Lovin' you could be so easy, lovin' you could make me warm'. *Osmonds Let me in*

2. 'You'll be my sunshine baby from L.A.'. *J. Osmond Long Haired Lover*

3. 'Are you hanging up a stocking on your wall, it's time that every Santa has a ball'. *Slade — Merry Xmas*

4. 'Back in 1780 when Bulgaria was a lad'. *Wombles*

5. 'You and I will be together, end of term until forever'.

6. 'Hello everyone, this is your action news reporter'. *R Stevens The Streak*

7. 'Did you think I would leave you dying when there's room on my horse for two?'. *R Harris Two Little Boys*

8. 'And yes I know how lonely life can be, the shadows follow me and night won't set me free'.

9. 'And the girl in the corner let no one ignore her, 'cause she thinks she's the passionate one'. *Sweet Ballroom Blitz*

10. 'They paved Paradise and put up a parking lot'. *Big Yellow Taxi Joni Mitchell*

26

ROUND 3: FAIRLY EASY

Weeny boppers

1. Can you identify this group from their Christian names: Merrill, Wayne, Donny, Alan and Jay?

2. Who sang CAN THE CAN and DEVIL GATE DRIVE?

3. Who took SUGAR BABY LOVE to the top of the charts?

4. What was Sweet Sensation's first hit called?

5. For which band was THIS TOWN AIN'T BIG ENOUGH FOR BOTH OF US a first hit?

6. Rearrange these words to form a well known song title: STOP STOP STOP.

7. How many records are there in the Top 20?

8. Who did the BANANA ROCK and then tried a MINUETTO ALLEGRETTO?

9. What was the name of the Swedish group who won the 1974 Eurovision Song Contest by singing WATERLOO?

10. Who had a No. 1 hit in 1971 with GRANDAD?

Teeny boppers

1. I DID WHAT I DID FOR MARIA he said in June 1971: who was he?

2. Who had hits with SCHOOL'S OUT, ELECTED and HALLO HURRAY? A. Cooper

3. Which French singer had a hit in 1970 with RAINDROPS KEEP FALLING ON MY HEAD?

4. What was the title of Edison Lighthouse's big hit at the beginning of 1970?

5. Which orchestra had a SHOWDOWN and said ROLL OVER BEETHOVEN?

6. Who starred in the films THAT'LL BE THE DAY and STARDUST? D. Essex

7. Radio 1 disc jockey Alan Freeman has a nickname: what is it? Fluff

8. Did Suzi Quatro sing about a 38, 58 or 48 CRASH?

9. Which band looked into a WISHING WELL, found a LITTLE BIT OF LOVE and declared that it was ALL RIGHT NOW? Free

10. Who used to sing with Paul Simon? A. g.

Teen-and-Twenties

1. Who said VIVA BOBBY JOE in 1969?

2. What song did Barry McGuire take into the Top 10 in 1965?

3. What was the title of Love Affair's first hit?

4. Which girl sang AS TEARS GO BY in 1964?

5. Who said I HEARD IT THROUGH THE GRAPE-VINE in 1969?

6. Hugo Montenegro was high in the charts in 1968 with a film theme: what was it called?

7. From which musical do these songs come: AQUARIUS, GOOD MORNING STARSHINE and LET THE SUN SHINE IN?

8. The McCoys had a big hit here in 1965: what was it called?

9. What was the Beatles' first film called?

10. True or false: songwriters Tony Hatch and Jackie Trent are husband and wife.

Mums and Dads

1. MAGIC MOMENTS, CATCH A FALLING STAR and DELAWARE were all hits for which American singer? *Perry Como*

2. Floyd Cramer had a hit with ON THE REBOUND in 1961: what instrument did he play on the record?

3. Who got to No. 2 in 1964 with RAG DOLL?

4. Who said I LIKE IT and wanted to know HOW DO YOU DO IT?

5. What was the Seekers' first hit called?

6. Was BOYS CRY a hit for Adam Faith, Eden Kane or John Leyton?

7. Mary Wells had a big hit in 1964: what was the song called?

8. Who sang I LOVE YOU BECAUSE in 1964?

9. Who said HOLD ME in 1964 and serenaded MARIA in 1965? *Cliff Richard*

10. Which singer do you associate with these songs: MOON-DREAMS, MAYBE BABY and OH BOY?

1. Who was known as the Forces' Sweetheart?

2. Which record label has as its trade mark a dog listening to a horn gramophone?

3. With which instrument do you associate Reginald Foorte, Reginald Dixon and Reginald Porter-Brown?

4. On which line was the wartime washing going to be hung out? *Seigfried Line*

5. Which American vocal group became famous for their imitations of musical instruments?

6. In which film was the song 42ND STREET featured?

7. Which of these song titles is correct: STARS FELL ON ALASKA, STARS FELL ON ALABAMA or STARS FELL ON ARKANSAS?

8. Who, in 1947, was asked to open the door?

9. Which American bandleader had a big hit with DARK TOWN POKER CLUB?

10. Who used to sing with guitarist Les Paul?

Which two Beatles' songs are shown here?

Fool on
the Hill

Helter
Skelter

Johnnie Walker's Maze

How many times can you pass through Johnnie Walker? It's not quite as gruesome as it sounds; all you have to do is to start in one corner of the square and mark out a route to the centre, spelling out 'Johnnie Walker' as many times as you can. Follow a continuous line, proceeding only horizontally or vertically and do not pass through any square more than once.

J	O	H	N	N	R	L	A	W	O	J
O	H	O	J	R	E	K	L	E	H	O
K	E	H	W	N	H	O	N	N	H	H
L	N	N	K	N	W	J	R	E	O	J
E	W	A	E	I	E	O	E	H	E	R
W	K	E	W	K	▓	R	K	E	K	L
R	E	R	A	L	K	E	L	E	E	A
J	O	H	L	E	E	L	A	E	E	W
H	R	N	N	W	I	E	W	N	N	H
O	H	W	L	A	N	N	H	I	O
J	O	H	K	E	R	J	O	H	O	J

Anagrams

Here is a further selection of anagrams and, like those on Page 18, each solution consists of only two words which may be the name of a singer, a group, a disc jockey or a song.

1. REEDS GROAN
2. STAIN SEEN SO WET
3. TRY GALE GRIT
4. JOIN WHERE LANK
5. NO GRUEL, VISIT BALL
6. HOT HEW
7. ROD BOOS VAIN GIT
8. FRY RYE BRAN
9. RIDE WET OVENS
10. FLESH IN A SPA

ROUND 4: STILL PRETTY SIMPLE

Weeny boppers

1. Who said MAKE ME SMILE (COME UP AND SEE ME) early in 1975?

2. Which month did Pilot sing about?

3. Who sang about SUGAR CANDY KISSES?

4. On which side of the mountain were Donny and Marie Osmond to be found?

5. Which of these songs was an Alvin Stardust hit: YOU YOU YOU, NA NA NA or STOP STOP STOP?

6. Who had a hit with KILLER QUEEN?

7. Which group includes Madam Cholet and Orinoco?

8. For which group was TELL HIM a first hit in 1974?

9. What did Disco Tex and the Sex-o-lettes want you to do?

10. On what medium wavelength is Radio 1 broadcast?

Teeny boppers

1. What was the title of the Pipkins' 1970 hit?

2. Did Chicory Tip sing GOOD GRIEF EDWINA, GOOD GRIEF GEORGINA or GOOD GRIEF CHRISTINA?

3. Who played the THEME FROM 'SHAFT'?

4. The Hollies once sang HE AIN'T HEAVY – HE'S MY – what?

5. Who was GONNA MAKE YOU AN OFFER YOU CAN'T REFUSE?

6. By what name was Peter Noone once known?

7. Which Jeff Beck hit was successfully reissued in 1972?

8. Who would you have found in TEMMA HARBOUR in 1970?

9. Who made a best-selling LP called DON'T SHOOT ME I'M ONLY THE PIANO PLAYER?

10. Who were noted for their SOLID GOLD EASY ACTION?

Teen-and-Twenties

1. What was the title of Mary Hopkin's first hit?

2. Whistling Jack Smith puckered up and blew himself into the charts in 1967: what was his tune?

3. Who was once KING OF THE ROAD? *Roger Miller*

4. Who went to No. 1 in 1966 with GREEN GREEN GRASS OF HOME?

5. What song did Keith West take into the charts in 1967?

6. Who produced a string of hits by the Ronettes and the Crystals? *Phil Spector*

7. What dance did Engelbert Humperdinck sing about in 1967?

8. Who sang about THE WINDMILLS OF YOUR MIND in 1969? *Noel Harrison*

9. Correct this statement: OH DEAR was a hit for Fleetwood Coat. *Mac*

10. With which song did Sandie Shaw win the 1967 Eurovision Song Contest?

Mums and Dads

1. Which girl singer enjoyed chart successes with DON'T TREAT ME LIKE A CHILD, YOU DON'T KNOW and WALKING BACK TO HAPPINESS?

2. What are the Christian names of the Everly Brothers?

3. What was the title of Tom Jones's first hit?

4. Who had a big hit with the theme song from the film TAMMY in 1957?

5. With which singer do you associate the song KISSES SWEETER THAN WINE?

6. Slim Dusty had a hit here in 1959: what was the song called?

7. Was BLUEBERRY HILL a hit for Fats Domino, Jerry Lee Lewis or Little Richard?

8. Who declared HERE COMES SUMMER in 1959?

9. Two singers had a hit with SINGING THE BLUES in 1956; Tommy Steele was one: who was the other?

10. For what unusual artist was DOMINIQUE a hit in 1963?

Grandparents

1. In which film did Judy Garland sing OVER THE RAIN-BOW?

2. Who had a hit with MUSIC! MUSIC! MUSIC! in 1950?

3. Complete this song title: IF I KNEW YOU WERE COMING . . .

4. Who had a very shiny nose?

5. Who had hits with TRULY, TRULY FAIR and BELLE, BELLE, MY LIBERTY BELLE?

6. What was the title of Glenn Miller's signature tune?

7. Who sang SUGAR BUSH and PICKIN' A CHICKEN?

8. Who do you associate with the song DONKEY SEREN-ADE?

9. Who invited us to TAKE THE A TRAIN?

10. Which singer was nicknamed the Velvet Fog?

Name the four groups represented by these drawings.

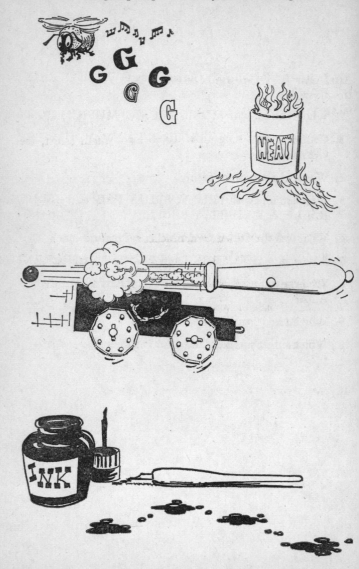

The Words

After your staggering success on Page 26, you should have no trouble at all in naming the ten songs from which these lines are taken.

1. 'The marching band came down along main street, the soldier blues fell in behind'.

2. 'Goodbye Norma Jean, though I never knew you at all'.

3. 'I remember April when the sun was in the sky and love was burning in your eyes'.

4. 'You come on like a dream, peaches and cream'.

5. 'There were funky Chinamen from funky Chinatown'.

6. 'Oh is he more too much more than a pretty face'.

7. 'Sheriff John Brown always hated me, for what I don't know'.

8. 'You fill up my senses like a night in the forest'.

9. 'When the snowman brings the snow'.

10. 'My friend Jack's got an ache in his back'.

Pop Codes

Can you break two simple codes? There are two sets of five coded song titles given below and, although the letters are in the correct order, they have been regrouped to conceal the true length of the words. See if you can find out what the song titles are: to help you, there's a clue with each code from which you should be able to crack it.

Code 1

Clue: R = E

1. GVRN LRYY BJEV OOBA

2. UBEFR JVGUA BANZR

3. ONP XFG NOO REF

4. FRNFB AFVAG URFHA

5. XVA TB SGU RE BNQ

Code 2

Clue: 8 = S

1. 20.22.7.12.21 21.12.21.14.2 24.15.12.6.23

2. 14.2.13.26 14.22.18.8 17.26.24.16

3. 7.18.14.22 18.8.7 18.20.19.7

4. 7.19.12.8 22.4 22.9.22.7 19.22 23.26.2.8

5. 26.4.19.18.7.22 9.8.19.26.23.22 12.21.11.26.15.22

ROUND 5: MEDIUM

Weeny boppers

1. What is the Christian name of the youngest Osmond brother?

2. Who said I WISH IT COULD BE CHRISTMAS EVERY DAY in the middle of a ROCK AND ROLL WINTER?

3. Correct this statement: AMAZING GLADYS was a hit for the Royal Scots Porage Oats.

4. Which French singer hit the top of the charts in 1974 with SHE?

5. Who had hits with DANCING ON A SATURDAY NIGHT and SCHOOL LOVE?

6. Which group features Noddy Holder as lead singer?

7. What song did Telly Savalas take to No. 1 in March 1975?

8. Which group's Christian names are Tito, Marlon, Michael, Jackie and Jermaine?

9. Who had a big hit with TWO LITTLE BOYS in 1969?

10. Who started a BALLROOM BLITZ?

Teeny boppers

1. Fleetwood Mac played a tune named after a bird: what was it called?

2. True or false: Michael Jackson's hit BEN was also the title of a film?

3. Who would you have found in MONTEGO BAY in 1970?

4. With whom do you connect Ziggy Stardust?

5. How are Richard and Karen Carpenter related?

6. Which British band made albums called HUMAN MENAGERIE and THE PSYCOMODO?

7. Who had a hit with DESIDERATA in 1972?

8. Clifford T. Ward had a hit with his first record: what was the song called?

9. Which leading rock star appeared in the films PERFORMANCE and NED KELLY?

10. Who sang HE'S GONNA STEP ON YOU AGAIN in 1971?

Teen-and-Twenties

1. True or false: Cilla Black's 1966 hit ALFIE was featured in the film of the same name?

2. Irish group Them, featuring Van Morrison, had two hits in 1965: can you name one of them?

3. Which group includes the three Gibb brothers?

4. Which Tamla Motown group were once DANCING IN THE STREET?

5. What was the title of Dave, Dee, Dozy, Beaky, Mick and Tich's first Top 10 hit?

6. With which group did the late Jim Morrison sing?

7. Which songwriter do you associate with the American group Bread?

8. I CAN'T LET MAGGIE GO has proved to be a nimble chart performer: which group sang the song?

9. Zager and Evans had a solitary hit in 1969: what was the title of their song?

10. In 1967 the Beatles made a film specially for television: what was it called?

Mums and Dads

1. Who asked ARE YOU SURE in 1961?

2. Until his untimely death, who was the Beatles' manager?

3. By what name is American singer Wayne Penniman better known?

4. Who serenaded JULIET in 1964?

5. With which group do you associate SHINDIG, ATLANTIS and THE RISE AND FALL OF FLINGEL BUNT?

6. Can you separate these three song titles which have been jumbled up together: YOU CATCH THE LOVE CRYING ROOM WHEN YOU DON'T WALK IN TO LET THE SUN TO KNOW YOU IS YOU.

7. What was the Kinks' first British hit called?

8. Who said LOVE IS LIKE A VIOLIN and then made PROMISES?

9. In which year did the Beatles have their first No. 1 hit?

10. By what name is Charles Eugene Boone better known?

Grandparents

1. Complete this orchestra's name: Les Brown and . . .

2. Which popular musical featured the song YOU ARE MY HEART'S DELIGHT?

3. Which bandleader ended his broadcasts by playing HERE'S TO THE NEXT TIME?

4. Supply the missing words in these song titles: I TOOK MY **** TO A PARTY, THE ***** CRAWLED UP THE WINDOW and LOVE IS THE ******** THING.

5. Who wrote the march KNIGHTSBRIDGE which was used to introduce the radio programme IN TOWN TO-NIGHT?

6. With which popular tenor do you most closely associate the song GIRLS WERE MADE TO LOVE AND KISS?

7. Who did Gracie Fields want to lead her to the altar?

8. Who, in 1954, sang DON'T LAUGH AT ME, 'CAUSE I'M A FOOL?

9. Which trumpeter scored a big success in 1954 with OH MY PAPA?

10. Who wanted you to LAY DOWN YOUR ARMS in 1956?

Popcross

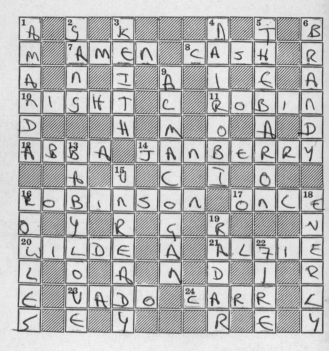

Across

7. Name changed for a group in the corner (4)

8. After Johnny comes money (4)

10. It meant fear for the Move (5)

11. Barry and Maurice are two: this is the third (5)

12. They met their Waterloo (4)

14. Dean Torrence's surfing partner (3, 5)

16. Smokey's missus? (8)

17. This number of times in Stevie's life (4)

20. Marty furious? Not quite (5)

21. Cilla asked if he knew what it was all about (5)

23. Add it to Via for Drupi's song (4)

24. It must be Vikki (4)

Down

1. She was serenaded by Stuart Gillies (6)

2. Gary was leader of it (4)

3. Greg, Carl – and someone else (5)

4. A colonial hit for Tommy Steele (7)

5. A noble disc jockey (3, 5)

6. A drink for Scott English (6)

9. She had a laugh in her voice – and bell bottom blues (4, 5)

13. Infant affection (4, 4)

15. Quite the opposite of what Frankie said you were (7)

16. If you only had time, you'd have John (6)

18. Don and Phil (6)

19. Palindromic love from Golden Earring (5)

22. Arthur Brown set the charts ablaze with this (4)

Name these two No. 1 hits from 1965.

ROUND 6: EVEN MORE MEDIUM

Weeny boppers

1. Which popular American group had hits with LET ME IN and LOVE ME FOR A REASON?

2. Which disc jockey is known as the Hairy Monster?

3. Who had a hit with MONSTER MASH?

4. Who said she was BORN WITH A SMILE ON MY FACE?

5. Which girl singer had hits with SUGAR ME and NO HONESTLY?

6. Correct this statement: MOULDY OLD PASTRY was a hit for Lieutenant Vulture.

7. What is the name of the tune that introduces the Radio 1 programme JUNIOR CHOICE?

8. What instrument does Bobby Crush play?

9. What tune was a big hit for the Simon Park Orchestra?

10. Who had a hit at the end of 1974 with YOU'RE THE FIRST, THE LAST, MY EVERYTHING?

Teeny boppers

1. Which group includes Ray Dorset in its line-up?

2. Waldo de Los Rios had a big hit in 1971 with a tune by which classical composer?

3. Melanie did well with a Rolling Stones song in November 1970: which one was it?

4. Was YOU'RE SO VAIN a hit for Carly Simon, Suzi Quatro or Carole King?

5. Which singer and songwriter made albums called TEA FOR THE TILLERMAN and BUDDHA AND THE CHOCOLATE BOX?

6. Who played the part of David Cassidy's mother in THE PARTRIDGE FAMILY?

7. The Jackson 5 had their first hit in February 1970: what was it called?

8. Which is right: HOT BUTTER by Popcorn or POP-CORN by Hot Butter?

9. What kind of child did the Detroit Spinners sing about?

10. Who, according to Ray Stevens, was Queen of the Blues?

Brigette the midget

Teen-and-Twenties

1. Which song-writing team have written hits for Mud, Sweet and Suzi Quatro?

2. They had a big hit with YESTERDAY'S GONE in 1968: can you remember the group's name?

3. What was Donovan's first hit called?

4. Which band originally consisted of Alan Price, John Steele, Chas Chandler, Hilton Valentine and Eric Burdon?

5. He wrote SUNNY and had a hit with it in 1966: who is he?

6. Who was lead singer with the Love Affair?

7. In which film was the Simon and Garfunkel song MRS ROBINSON featured?

8. Messrs Young, Cliff and Jones share the same Christian name: what is it?

9. Who was noted for her medicinal compound?

10. SATURDAY CLUB was a long-running BBC pop programme: who compèred it for most of its run?

Mums and Dads

1. Which group made the charts with IF YOU GOTTA MAKE A FOOL OF SOMEBODY, I'M TELLING YOU NOW and YOU WERE MADE FOR ME?

2. Who had a hit with IT'S MY PARTY in 1963?

3. What was Cilla Black's first Top 20 hit called?

4. Peter, Paul and Mary had a hit here in 1963 with a Bob Dylan song: what was it called?

5. Who played THE GAME OF LOVE in 1965?
   Wayne Fontana + Mindbenders

6. Who used to introduce the BBC's Tuesday lunchtime programme POP INN?

7. What is the name of the vocal group who sang on many of Elvis Presley's records?

8. Who was ON THE BEACH in August 1964?

9. Heinz had a hit in 1963 that was a tribute to a famous rock 'n' roll singer: what was it called?

10. With what song did Bob Lind have a hit in 1966?

Grandparents

1. YOU'RE DANCING ON MY HEART is the signature tune of which dance band leader?

2. From which musical does the song KANSAS CITY come?

3. Who wrote the popular tune CHEROKEE?

4. NELLIE THE ELEPHANT was made popular by a child star: what was her name?

5. From which musical do these songs come: THE GIRL THAT I MARRY, ANYTHING YOU CAN DO and DOIN' WHAT COMES NATUR'LLY?

6. Which veteran actress and singer do you associate with the song VITALITY?

7. What was the name of Tommy Dorsey's musical brother?

8. Which tune do you associate with the band led by Charlie Barnet?

9. What instrument does Count Basie play? Piano

10. Who made a hit out of I CAN'T GET STARTED?

Two more Tamla-Motown hits – give the titles.

Anagrams

Here is a further selection of anagrams for your continued aggravation and these are more difficult than those on pages 18 and 34.

1. I BITE THAT HEATH REAR
2. O LORD I HAVE STALE MAID
3. DOUSE HIGH LIT NOSE
4. O MORE PORKERS
5. STIR BOY CLEARLY
6. HANDY ACTS AID GROANING NUT
7. MEAL MEN NEAR DARK SLOPE
8. BUT THUS I GAIN EVERY LIFE
9. RIVET TIN COOP FOR ANN
10. HAD MAD TIN VIOL

Label Square

The names of 38 record labels are concealed in this square. They read horizontally, vertically and diagonally, both forwards and backwards.

```
K D X Q R E S I R P E R Z V S
C E K J A M W H A R V E S T I
A C A P I T O L D L N N Q N L
R C C U B E C N B F M R H O A
T A B T M S B E U E A A G D S
R P S E U T A Y S M R W T N Y
O S P I L I H P K I E B A O R
J D M P O L Y D O R D N P L H
A Y R U C R E M X B A V T T C
N L D N A L S I S T A X R E H
E F H M E B R U N S W I C K L
L J S K Q E O O H F R I M C A
P N T M U J F G T S P C K O N
P R Z A O G I T R E V K A R L
A V A M S I R A H C S B D E P
```

ROUND 7: SO YOU THINK YOU'RE DOING WELL?

Weeny boppers

1. Who had a hit with NICE ONE CYRIL?

2. Which American singer had a big hit with ROCK YOUR BABY?

3. The Osmonds have a singing sister: what is her name?

4. Correct this statement: SPOTLIGHT was a hit for David Sussex.

5. Is heavy music a pile of 78s, another name for progressive pop or songs like CARRY THAT WEIGHT and FOURTEEN TONS?

6. Who had a hit with HEY THERE (LONELY GIRL) in 1974?

7. What was Cockney Rebel's first hit called?

8. Lulu is Scottish: is her real name Agnes Auchtermuchty, Marie Lawrie or Kenneth McKellar?

9. Who sang CHIRPY CHIRPY CHEEP CHEEP in 1971?

10. Complete this group's name: Harold Melvin and . . . ?

Teeny boppers

1. In which band would you find brothers Ron and Russell Mael?

2. Who made a hit LP called HERGEST RIDGE?

3. What was the title of K.C. and the Sunshine Band's first hit?

4. What kind of boy did Nazareth sing about?

5. With what kind of music do you associate the name Jim Reeves?

6. Complete this song title: CRYING, LAUGHING . . . ?

7. Two singers teamed up in 1971 and had a hit with ROSETTA: who were they?

8. Who sang DID YOU EVER with Nancy Sinatra?

9. Who had hits with PICK UP THE PIECES and BURN BABY BURN?

10. Was BIG YELLOW TAXI a hit for Judy Collins, Joni Mitchell or Joan Baez?

Teen-and-Twenties

1. What was Jonathan King's first hit called?

2. Who sang an ODE TO BILLIE JOE?

3. Donovan and Jeff Beck combined to make a hit record in 1969: what was it called?

4. True or false: the Beatles once had a drummer called Pete Best?

5. RESCUE ME she pleaded in 1965: who was she?

6. Hugh Grundy, Paul Atkinson, Chris White, Rod Argent and Colin Blunstone were the original members of which group?

7. The title, please, of Thunderclap Newman's 1969 hit?

8. Who had CARELESS HANDS in 1967?

9. Who used to introduce the Radio 1 programme SCENE AND HEARD?

10. Who was lead singer with hit-making group Amen Corner?

Mums and Dads

1. Who had hits with REBEL ROUSER, SOME KINDA EARTHQUAKE and SHAZAM?

2. Which duo made a record called HARLEM SHUFFLE?

3. Who had a hit with IN THE MIDNIGHT HOUR in 1965?

4. What was the title of Amen Corner's first hit?

5. At one time the Beatles acted as backing group for an English singer working in Germany: what was his name?

6. Immersed in DEEP PURPLE in 1963 and WHISPERING in 1964 were – who?

7. Who dealt a DECK OF CARDS in 1959 and again in 1963?

8. From which film did Elvis Presley's hit JAILHOUSE ROCK come?

9. WORLD WITHOUT LOVE was Peter and Gordon's first hit in 1964: who wrote the song?

10. What was the BBC's first television pop show called?

1. Which famous musical was based on the book ANNA AND THE KING OF SIAM?

2. Which internationally famous singer and actor began his recording career as vocalist with the Tommy Dorsey Orchestra?

3. True or false: Band leader Bob Crosby is Bing Crosby's brother?

4. Who was known as the King of Jazz?

5. 'Hutch' was a popular performer in the 1940s and 1950s: what was his real name?

6. Complete this band's name: Spike Jones and . . .

7. With which band did Tex Beneke play before forming his own orchestra?

8. Which song was strongly featured in the film CASABLANCA?

9. What is a pianola?

10. By what name was Gerald Bright better known?

Two songs connected with transport – can you name them?

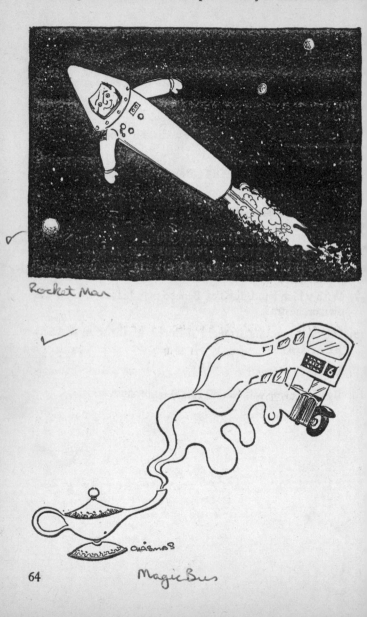

Rocket Man

Magic Bus

Who are we?

Similar to the puzzle on page 17, this one is a little more complicated as there are *two* names to be found. Each line gives you a clue to two letters and, when you have discovered what they are, rearrange them to form the names of a couple of American singers.

Our first is in NEAR and also in PINE   N E

Our second is in YELP and also in GREY   Y E

Our third is in LAVA and also in VOLE   V L

Our fourth is in SING and also in SLIT   S I

Our fifth is in TANK and also in NOTE   N T

Our sixth is in ROPE and also in PART   R P

Our seventh is in ALLY and also in TRAY   Y A

Our eighth is in PART and also in CRAM

Our ninth is in CHEF and also in NICE

Our tenth is in LINT and also in PAIN

Our eleventh is in SOLE and also in LAST

Our twelfth is in VASE and also in SALT

More lyrics

A third selection of lines from well-known songs for you to identify. Can you name the singer and the song in each case?

1. 'Strands of light upon a bedroom floor, change the night through an open door'. *Marouse KJ*

2. 'You're a child of sweet sixteen, never made the big town scene'. *Angle Free GB.*

3. 'Now I don't mean to be a stick in the dirt, the world is changin' only in reverse'. *Burn Baby Burn A 7 -*

4. 'You sheltered me from harm, kept me warm, kept me warm'. *Everything Tower Ken Boathe*

5. 'Some call me Arnie, some call me Slim'. *T. Rex Groover*

6. 'Honey though I think about you day and night'.

7. 'Mama take this badge off me, I can't use it any more'. *Knocking on Heaven's door BD.*

8. 'I was walking down the High Street when I heard foot-steps behind me'. *The Laughing Gnome D.B*

9. 'Well everybody knows down Ladbroke Grove, you have to leap across the street'. *Leo Sayer*

10. 'They asked me how I knew my true love was true'. *Smoke gets in your eyes*

ROUND 8: GETTING TOUGHER

Weeny boppers

1. What was Cozy Powell's first hit called?

2. Who sang about a HONALOOCHIE BOOGIE and then said ROLL AWAY THE STONE?

3. Which American actor had a No. 1 hit with WANDRIN' STAR in 1970?

4. Who was ALONE AGAIN (NATURALLY)?

5. Rearrange these words to form a well-known song title: IN I'M IT COULD BE FALLING LOVE.

6. Who had a hit in 1974 with ROCK ME GENTLY?

7. With which city do you associate the Beatles?

8. What song did Shag take into the Top 10 in November 1972?

9. THERE ARE MORE QUESTIONS THAN ANSWERS was a hit in 1972: who for?

10. Here are the titles of three 1975 hits jumbled up together. Can you separate them? HELLO I SAID PLEASE KEEP THE GOOD LOVE SECRETS THAT YOU TELL HIM THAT CAN NEVER DIE.

Teeny boppers

1. Which band sang about a HORSE WITH NO NAME at the beginning of 1972? *America*

2. Who made LPs entitled THESE FOOLISH THINGS and ANOTHER TIME, ANOTHER PLACE?

3. GOODBYE SAM, HELLO – who? sang Cliff Richard.

4. Who had a hit with ME AND YOU AND A DOG NAMED BOO in 1971? *Lobo*

5. In which year did Radio 1 start?

6. Which is right: TITANIC was a hit for Sultana or SULTANA was a hit for Titanic?

7. Messrs Ball, Lynch and Rogers share the same Christian name: what is it? *Kenny*

8. What do the initials BBC stand for?

9. SWEET TALKING GUY was successfully reissued in 1972: who sang the song?

10. What was the title of Mr Bloe's 1970 hit?

Groovin with Mr. Bloe

Teen-and-Twenties

1. Who sang OH HAPPY DAY in 1969?

2. Whose first hit was titled I'M INTO SOMETHING GOOD?

3. Which country does Dana come from?

4. In 1966, did Peter and Gordon have a hit with LADY MADONNA, LADY GODIVA or LADY WILL-POWER?

5. What day of the week did the Mamas and the Papas sing about in 1966? *Monday*

6. True or false: In March 1968 Donovan had a hit with JENNIFER ECCLES? *False*

7. Which group includes brothers Ray and Dave Davies in its line-up? *Kinks*

8. Who sang THE BOAT THAT I ROW in 1967?

9. Which influential British band recorded these LPs: SAUCERFUL OF SECRETS, UMMAGUMMA and OBSCURED BY CLOUDS?

10. With which group does Reg Presley sing?

Mums and Dads

1. Who had hits with BIRD DOG, 'TIL I KISSED YOU and BYE BYE LOVE?

2. Who wanted to CALL UP THE GROUPS in 1964?

3. What was the Beatles' first Top 20 hit called?

4. What song did the Cascades take into the Top 10 in 1963?

5. Who was a TOWER OF STRENGTH in 1961?

6. Which TV pop show did Brian Matthew used to introduce?

7. What is Ringo Starr's real name?

8. Which singer appeared in these films: SERIOUS CHARGE, EXPRESSO BONGO and TWO A PENNY?

9. A bell for a hit and a klaxon for a miss: what TV programme featured these sounds?

10. What was Cat Stevens's first record called?

Grandparents

1. He sang with Roy Fox, Geraldo and Ray Noble among many others and died in a land-mine blast in 1941. Who was he?

2. Supply the missing words in these song titles: WHEN IT'S ---------- IN THE ROCKIES, WALKIN' MY ---- BACK HOME and I COVER THE ----------.

3. Who sang DANCING ON THE CEILING in the film EVERGREEN?

4. With which American bandleader do you associate the tune THE PEANUT VENDOR?

5. Who had a big hit with THIS OLE HOUSE? Was it Dinah Shore, Rosemary Clooney or Peggy Lee?

6. By what name is Doris Kappelhoff better known?

7. Who do you associate with these songs: SING AS WE GO, WISH ME LUCK (AS YOU WAVE ME GOOD-BYE) and SALLY?

8. Who was known as the Brazilian Bombshell?

9. Which British bandleader uses IN THE MOOD as his theme tune?

10. What were the christian names of the Andrews sisters?

Quizzigram

Solve the clues given below and put the answers in the diagram with the first letter of each word in the left-hand column. When these letters are rearranged, they will give you the name of a famous British pop musician.

1. Sunday morning pop once (4, 4)
2. Country and western teens? (9)
3. They had the right (10)
4. Michelle helped them to the top (11)
5. Let there be Sandy (6)
6. Integrated band (6)
7. The cost of Alan (5)
8. Inviting singers (11)
9. Is he a downer? Not after a reshuffle (6)
10. Nearly seekers (9)
11. Swirling guitarist (4)
12. The sunshine superman (7)
13. Windy lot (8)

Remember when?

How good is your memory for hits? Here is a list of ten hit records: see if you can recall the year in which they made the charts.

1. GALVESTON by Glen Campbell

2. SEE MY BABY JIVE by Wizzard

59 3. IT DOESN'T MATTER ANYMORE by Buddy Holly

4. MAKE IT EASY ON YOURSELF by the Walker Brothers

70 5. FUNNY FUNNY by the Sweet

6. YOU'RE DRIVING ME CRAZY by the Temperance Seven

7. DON'T THROW YOUR LOVE AWAY by the Searchers

8. EVERYTHING IS BEAUTIFUL by Ray Stevens

9. I WANT TO HOLD YOUR HAND by the Beatles

69 10. A WHITER SHADE OF PALE by Procol Harum

ROUND 9: HARD

Weeny boppers

1. Who sang GOOD OLD ARSENAL in 1971?

2. Which newcomer hit No. 3 in 1972 with YOU'RE A LADY?

3. Which American group had a hit with HERE I GO AGAIN in 1972?

4. Who sang about a YEAR OF DECISION and then asked WHEN WILL I SEE YOU AGAIN?

5. With what song did Marie Osmond have her first British hit?

6. Which teenybopper favourite reached No. 3 with ROCKIN' ROBIN in June 1972?

7. By what name is Priscilla White better known?

8. Who sang about LILY THE PINK?

9. Who had a hit with NEANDERTHAL MAN in 1970?

10. What is the name of the Who's drummer?
    Hotlegs

    Keith Moon

Teeny boppers

1. What piece of music by Richard Strauss was made into a hit by Deodato?

2. SAY YOU DON'T MIND was a hit here in March 1972: who sang the song?

3. With which American city do you associate the Tamla Motown label?

4. Which former pop star manages Leo Sayer?

5. HMV is a famous record label: what do the initials HMV stand for? *His Masters Voice.*

6. Which American girl singer once released an LP called TAPESTRY? ✓

7. Which group said I'M DOING FINE NOW in 1973?

8. Which of these is right: Tim Lloyd and Andrew Rice-Webber, Tim Rice and Andrew Lloyd-Webber or Tim Webber and Andrew Lloyd-Rice?

9. On which LP did these songs appear: LOVELY RITA, FIXING A HOLE and BEING FOR THE BENEFIT OF MR KITE?

10. The soundtrack of the film BUTCH CASSIDY AND THE SUNDANCE KID produced a big hit song: what was it? *Raindrops*

Teen-and-Twenties

1. Who exactly were the people referred to in Marvin Gaye's 1970 hit ABRAHAM, MARTIN AND JOHN?

2. Two groups had hits with OB LA DI, OB LA DA: one was Marmalade but what was the other group called? *Beatles*

3. The Dave Clark Five once starred in a feature film: what was it called?

4. What is Donovan's surname?

5. Who wrote ANOTHER SATURDAY NIGHT which was revived by Cat Stevens in 1974?

6. Who showed us how to WALK TALL and then asked WHAT WOULD I BE?

7. By what name is American singer and songwriter Robert Zimmerman better known?

8. Who was OUT OF TIME in July 1966? *Stones*

9. Which band made an LP called SELLING ENGLAND BY THE POUND? *Genesis*

10. Honey Lantree was a rarity – a girl drummer. For which group did she lay down the beat?

Mums and Dads

1. What was the title of the Kinks' second hit, which made the Top 10 in 1964?

2. This strange sentence contains three song titles: what are they? AS YOU BRING ME THE LONG WORLD TRADE HOME TO ME FOR HE NEEDS IT ON AS I WOULDN'T.

3. Chris Curtis, John McNally, Mike Pender and Tony Jackson were members of which group?

4. What is the name of Elvis Presley's manager?

5. He produced hits by Heinz, the Tornados and the Honeycombs and died in tragic circumstances: who was he?

6. What is Tommy Steele's real name?

7. In their early days in Liverpool the Beatles often played in a famous club: what was it called?

8. Who did Gordon Waller used to sing with?

9. Ned Miller had a solitary British hit in 1963: what was it called?

10. Which group had a hit in 1964 with a song called TELL ME WHEN?

Grandparents

1. Although known primarily as a bandleader, Glenn Miller was also an instrumentalist: what did he play?

2. Who wrote the novelty song RHYMES, which was popular in the 1930s?

3. 'Flotsam and Jetsam' were a popular duo on stage, the radio and records: what were their real names?

4. Which distinguished author wrote the lyric for the song A NICE CUP OF TEA, made popular by Binnie Hale?

5. For which film did Richard Addinsell write his WARSAW CONCERTO?

6. Which comedian used his own song CONFIDEN-TIALLY as his signature tune?

7. Who led a band called Pieces of Eight?

8. Which musical told the story of a Scottish village that only appeared once every hundred years?

9. With whose orchestra did Ella Fitzgerald record A TISKET, A TASKET early on in her career?

10. Which American band leader had a College of Musical Knowledge?

Two songs to do with forms of transport – can you give the titles?

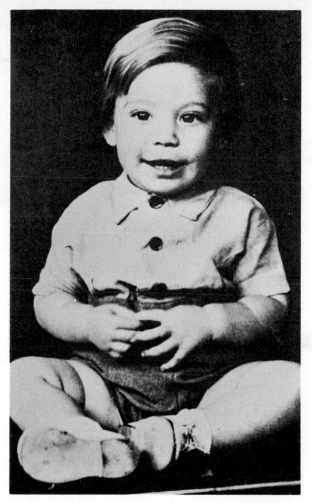

Can you identify this baby who is now a famous drummer?

A

B

C

On this page are three
male pop stars and
opposite are the girls
with whom they
teamed up. Can you
pair them off
correctly?

X

Y

Z

Here, and on the next two pages, are pictures of
three well-known groups. Can you name the
missing face in each one ?

A

B

These singers also
play an instrument:
but which one?

C

7

Here are two familiar faces of today's pop scene;
but what names did they use to record under?

A

B

C

Three famous faces:
can you name their
famous brothers?

A

B

Each of these singers
left a well-known
group: which one in
each case?

C

Johnnie Walker, the David Bailey of West
London, has been pointing his Brownie at these
five lovely ladies. They are all married to one of
the pop stars shown on the next few pages: can
you decide who is married to whom?

Pop Codes

Two more codes for you to break, both more difficult than those on page 42. In this letter code, the answers are all the names of groups. The words are in the proper order and the lengths are correct but the letters of each word have been rearranged before coding. This means that if after decoding you get FLCIF RHIRCAD NAD EHT SWODHSA the answer would be CLIFF RICHARD AND THE SHADOWS. Although this code follows a formal pattern, each line must be dealt with separately, since what applies in one line may not necessarily fit elsewhere. Your clue: H or G can equal S.

1. WLZSIO REVNNM LYV RGU TMYF SKKFH
2. VPNHLB MGRKIYIJ WZK USG FOYQMHXT
3. ORYNB Q INIIPZV WMY SUG XLWVOFH
4. SGV FLUI HKZUGFM
5. WLSVGIYKRHJ UI ZNM

This numerical code, although it may look involved, is based on a simple four-stage operation and the answers are all album titles. The word lengths are correct but the order of the words and the letters within them have been rearranged before coding. To start you on your way, this clue: 521 = B.

1. 221.701.811.621.411.711.801.811.801 811.421.621.-
   801.701.311.621 801.601.221.901.011.221.701
   811.911.701.811.901.
2. 321.511.211.521 301.621.801.811 801.621
   501.221.211.511.
3. 701.801.411.601 801.021.311.701.811.911
   621.801.801.111 511.621.511.
4. 121.211 811.321.221.801 911.701.221
   901.611.321.621 211.311.411.211.
5. 901.701.221.421.311.601.201 221.911.701
   411.901.421.811.221 121.211.

Anagram's

Here is a further selection of anagrams which, as before, are a mixture of artists, disc jockeys and song titles.

1. BELT ROY HE RIGHT DEMON

2. YES, HE TILTS HER ORB

3. DEMON ON SLED

4. TROLL WON DRINK RACE

5. FAT ADA WORKING THE BROWN CHEESE HALL

6. LIVE CRANE CRAVED TREACLE EWER

7. MEMO: DON'T GO BERT FERRET

8. HUNT DEAF GOLDEN AXE

9. ANN FEAR MALE

10. A VET'S SCENT

ROUND 10: VERY HARD

Weeny boppers

1. What was Showaddywaddy's first hit called?

2. Who sang about SEASONS IN THE SUN in 1974?

3. Who sang the PUSHBIKE SONG?

4. Who went to No. 1 with BABY JUMP in 1971?

5. Which band had hits with BROKEN DOWN ANGEL and THIS FLIGHT TONIGHT?

6. Was BEG STEAL OR BORROW a hit for the Newbcats, the New Seekers or the New Vaudeville Band?

7. Which of these titles is the odd one out: SHE LOVES YOU, I FEEL FINE, THE LAST TIME and ELEANOR RIGBY?

8. Who had a No. 1 hit with I'M STILL WAITING in 1971?

9. Who were once STUCK IN THE MIDDLE WITH YOU?

10. Who said HOLD YOUR HEAD UP in March 1972?

Teeny boppers

1. Which group was in our Top 20 with RAG MAMA RAG in 1970?

2. Which song-writer and producer is responsible for the Wombles' records? *Mike Batt*.

3. Who had a hit with PATCHES in 1970?

4. Are there seven, three or five people in the Detroit Emeralds?

5. What was the title of Gary Glitter's second hit?

6. Which member of the Jackson 5 made an album called COME INTO MY LIFE?

7. She sang COME WHAT MAY in the 1972 Eurovision Song Contest and won it. Who is she?

8. Which film star was Elton John singing about on CANDLE IN THE WIND?

9. Which band consists of Les Gray, Dave Mount, Rob Davis and Ray Stiles?

10. What is Rosko's real name?

Teen-and-Twenties

1. Which American group released LPs with wholesome titles like HOT RATS and WEASELS RIPPED MY FLESH?

2. Who had a big hit with SABRE DANCE in 1969?

3. Which singer starred in the film ALICE'S RES-TAURANT?

4. A saucy record by Jane Birkin and Serge Gainsbourg created a lot of fuss in 1969: what was it called?

5. Which Beatle played the part of Gripweed in HOW I WON THE WAR? *John Lennon.*

6. The Who had their first hit in 1965: what was it called? *Can't Explain*

7. Which British girl had a small hit with ANNIVERSARY WALTZ in 1968?

8. Brenton Wood had a solitary hit in 1968: what was the song called?

9. What was the first record to be played on Radio 1? *Flowers in the Rain Move.*

10. Paul and Barry Ryan had their first hit in 1965: what was it called?

Mums and Dads

1. Who led a group called the Rebel Rousers?

2. Which of these Elvis Presley hits was *not* also the title of a film: JAILHOUSE ROCK, VIVA LAS VEGAS, BLUE CHRISTMAS and KISSIN' COUSINS?

3. By what name is Ronald Wycherley better known?

4. Hank Marvin, Bruce Welch and Tony Meehan were three of the original Shadows: who was the fourth?

5. What was the Rolling Stones' first Top 20 hit called?

6. Who produced the popular television show OH BOY?

7. Jim Reeves once made a film in South Africa: what was it called?

8. Which well-known television personality had a minor hit with THE SHIFTING, WHISPERING SANDS in 1956?

9. Which popular pianist used to play rags and boogies on her 'other' piano?

10. Jazzman Chris Barber had an instrumental hit in 1959: what was it called?

Grandparents

1. Who wrote the popular song MAYBE IT'S BECAUSE I'M A LONDONER?

2. From which musical do these songs come: A BUSHEL AND A PECK, FUGUE FOR TIN HORNS and LUCK BE A LADY?

3. With which bandleader did you swing and sway?

4. Complete this orchestra's name: Shep Fields and . . . ?

5. With what instrument do you principally associate Lionel Hampton?

6. What was Duke Ellington's real name?

7. How many Smith Brothers were there?

8. In which film, in which his co-star was Bing Crosby, did Fred Astaire perform PUTTIN' ON THE RITZ?

9. Who regretted that she was unable to lunch today?

10. Which song did Bing Crosby adopt as his signature tune?

Name the film and the record album illustrated by these cartoons.

Lyrics again

A fourth selection of lyrics from songs which have been hits at one time. Once again, can you identify the title of the song and the singer or group who made it into a hit?

1. 'Well it's one for the money, two for the show, three to get ready, now go cat go'. _Blue Suede Shoes_ ✓

2. 'The weather here has been as nice as it can be, although it doesn't really matter much to me'. _You Wear It Well R5_ ✓

3. 'When the moon is in the seventh house and Jupiter aligns with Mars'. _Aquarius - from Hair_ ✓

4. 'I felt the knife in my hand and she laughed no more'. _Delilah - T. Jones - SAHB_ ✓

5. 'Father Mackenzie writing the words of a sermon that no one will hear'. _Elanor Rigby - Beatles_

6. 'My folks were always putting him down, they said he came from the wrong side of town'. _Leader of the Pack - Shangrilas_

7. 'I may not always love you but as long as there are stars above you'. _God Only Knows Beach Boys_

8. 'When I was a little girl I had a rag doll, only doll I ever owned'. _River Deep, Mountain High - Ike & Tina Turner_

9. 'Ground control to Major Tom, take your protein pills and put your helmet on'. _Space Oddity - D. Bowie_

10. 'Look out the left the captain said, the lights down there that's where we'll land'. _Last Flight Tonight - Nazareth._

Double-cross

When you have solved the clues given in the first puzzle, the letters in column A will spell out the name of a well-known group. Transfer the letters in the puzzle to the grid below and you will get a line from one of their most popular songs.

1. Syrup (7)

2. Indians (6)

3. Radiated (7)

4. Smashes (6)

5. Deserving (7)

6. Weapon store (7)

7. Secure (3); Roman way (3)

8. Vulgar (3); Lout (3)

9. Serious (7)

10. Wrench (6)

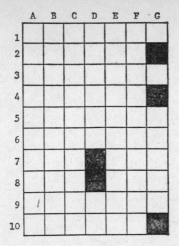

	A	B	C	D	E	F	G
1							
2							■
3							
4							■
5							
6							
7				■			
8				■			
9	/						
10							■

10B	3C	1E	7A	2E	9C	7C	■	6G	8B	6E	5C	4F	1G	8A	8G
7F	9D	■	5B	■	4A	8E	1D	9G	■	6D	2C				
4D	■	10C	5E	7E	9A	1B	■	8C	2B	3D	2A				
1A	9B	10F	5G	3F	6B	7B	5D	9E	■	3E	6F	4C	3A	9F	
6A	5F	3G	■	6C	10D	4B	3B	7G	1F	8F	2D	5A			
10A	4E	10E	1C	2F											

ROUND 11: GENIUSES ONLY

Weeny boppers

1. Scottish teenager Neil Reid went to No. 2 with his first record: what was its title?

2. Who had a No. 1 hit with VINCENT in 1972?

3. Who sang YOU WEAR IT WELL in 1972?

4. Which three-piece band had a hit with RESURRECTION SHUFFLE?

5. Which band had hits with TAP TURNS ON THE WATER and WALKING in 1971?

6. Who sang about THE MOST BEAUTIFUL GIRL from BEHIND CLOSED DOORS?

7. Who had a SILVER MACHINE in 1972?

8. What was Alvin Stardust's second hit called?

9. I'M GONNA RUN AWAY FROM YOU was a hit in 1971: who for?

10. Which American band had a hit with SEVEN SEAS OF RHYE?

Teeny boppers

1. Which band consists of Alan Merrill, Jake Hooker and Paul Varley?

2. Which American band was COMIN' HOME in 1970?

3. With which group did Peter Doyle used to sing?

4. Who had a hit with BRANDY in 1971?

5. In which controversial film was Mike Oldfield's TUBULAR BELLS used as incidental music?

6. HARE KRISHNA MANTRA was an unusual Top 20 entry in 1969: who performed the song?

7. Which two members of Slade wrote their hit EVERY-DAY?

8. Who was in our Top 20 in 1972 with SUZANNE BE-WARE OF THE DEVIL?

9. Which Pete Townshend song was a hit for the New Seekers?

10. Who had a hit with a *revival* of SUGAR SUGAR in 1971?

Teen-and-Twenties

1. The Show Stoppers had a solitary hit in 1968: what was their song called?

2. By what name are John Stokes, Con Cluskey and Dec Cluskey better known?

3. What is the name of Johnny Cash's wife?

4. Which celebrated guitarist formed a group called Derek and the Dominoes?

5. Which title is the odd one out here: APACHE, WHEELS, DIZZY and ALBATROSS?

6. By what name was Engelbert Humperdinck once known?

7. Which hit song featured in the film MIDNIGHT COW-BOY?

8. At one time Peter Noone appeared in a long-running TV series: which one?

9. Can you name the Moody Blues' first hit?

10. In which Beatles' film was the song YOU'RE GONNA LOSE THAT GIRL first heard?

Mums and Dads

1. Who sang about SEVEN LITTLE GIRLS in 1959?

2. Whose first hit was called DIANA?

3. Who else died in the plane crash that killed Buddy Holly?

4. Who represented Great Britain in the 1959 Eurovision Song Contest with SING LITTLE BIRDIE?

5. Was TEQUILA a hit for the Ramrods, the Champs or the String-a-longs?

6. American record producer Terry Melcher is the son of which actress and singer?

7. Supply the missing words in these Craig Douglas hits: A HUNDRED ------ OF CLAY, WHEN MY LITTLE GIRL IS ------- and PRETTY ---- EYES.

8. Bobby Darin had a minor hit here with SPLISH SPLASH in 1958 but it was also a Top 10 hit for a British comedian: which one?

6. American record producer Terry Melcher is the son of 1958?

10. Where was Elvis Presley born?

Grandparents

1. In which film did Marlene Dietrich sing FALLING IN LOVE AGAIN?

2. What was Judy Garland's real name?

3. Which British songwriter wrote RED SAILS IN THE SUNSET, SOUTH OF THE BORDER and HARBOUR LIGHTS?

4. Who played the part of Al Jolson in the films THE JOLSON STORY and JOLSON SINGS AGAIN?

5. What is the alternative title of the song PERFIDIA?

6. Who sang the original German version of LILI MARLENE?

7. Who sang THE TENEMENT SYMPHONY in the Marx Brothers' film THE BIG STORE?

8. From which show does WE'LL GATHER LILACS come?

9. In which of Walt Disney's cartoon films was the song WHO'S AFRAID OF THE BIG BAD WOLF introduced?

10. To which popular actress and singer is Phil Harris married?

Anagrams

A final selection of anagrams for you to play around with which, like those earlier in the book, are an assortment of names and song titles.

1. LIVE SPY LEERS

2. SHE TORE GRANT'S HAMS

3. CHOSE THE BABY

4. A GIN WITH THIS TENNIS

5. YOU MAKE GREENS FACE YOUR FAT NOON FAUN

6. PROD THIS CREEP, SAVE GUN

7. CLIFF FAN DIED SO EAT WHOLE DOOR

8. BEEP MEN SHAMED

9. THEY CROW A TUNE TO FAT SID

10. NUT RAN BY BLOCK

Quizzigram

A third puzzle which, when you have solved the clues and re-arranged the first letters of each answer (which should be written in the left-hand column), will produce the name of an influential pop personality.

1. Perhaps *you* can get some (12)
2. Off-hand band (7)
3. Was January magic for them? (5)
4. Reset N-n-noel for a Beatle (6)
5. Prickly singer? (5)
6. Put pep into becoming a marionette (6)
7. Dream about this album (7)
8. Love that never ended (11)
9. He couldn't hear his opera (5)
10. Brothers this good (9)
11. I. Robson wants to be like Roy (7)

ROUND 12: OKAY, CLEVERSTICKS, TRY THIS

Weeny boppers

1. Who got to No. 1 with TEARS OF A CLOWN in 1970?

2. Which band had hits with PYJAMARAMA and STREET LIFE?

3. Who were STANDING IN THE ROAD in September 1972?

4. Who made LPs called ALL THINGS MUST PASS and LIVING IN THE MATERIAL WORLD?

5. Who went to No. 3 in 1971 with JOHNNY REGGAE?

6. Which group had hits with PAINT IT BLACK, GET OFF OF MY CLOUD and JUMPING JACK FLASH?

7. Which trio had hits with SISTER JANE in 1972 and TOM TOM TURNAROUND in 1971?

8. Put the missing words in these song titles: ME AND ----- DOWN BY THE SCHOOL YARD, BORN WITH A ----- ON MY FACE and WHO'S IN THE ---------- PATCH WITH SALLY.

9. Who sang ANOTHER DAY in 1971?

10. Paul, Jack and Tom share the same surname: what is it?

Teeny boppers

1. Which girl singer was born in the Tiger Bay area of Cardiff?

2. Who took a reggae treatment of BLACK PEARL into the Top 20 in 1970?

3. With which hit-making group is Barry Hay lead vocalist?

4. Is Judge Dread's real name David Jones, Alex Hughes or Clive Powell?

5. What song did Nicky Thomas take into the Top 20 in 1970?

6. What is Melanie's full name?

7. Who wrote the music for the film O LUCKY MAN?

8. What combination of Tamla groups had a No. 3 hit in 1969 with I'M GONNA MAKE YOU LOVE ME?

9. Which disc jockey made a brief appearance on Lynsey de Paul's record WON'T SOMEBODY DANCE WITH ME?

10. Who sang WHO DO YOU LOVE in 1970?

Teen-and-Twenties

1. Chet Atkins is a famous American musician: what instrument does he play?

2. Jack Bruce and Eric Clapton were two members of Cream: who was the third?

3. Shirley Ellis had a solitary British hit in 1965: what was the song called?

4. Which DJ once had a Saturday afternoon show on BBC radio called WHERE IT'S AT?

5. What was the name of the girl who sang with the *original* Seekers?

6. Which London Underground station did the New Vaudeville Band sing about in June 1967?

7. Which American artist made albums called AXIS BOLD AS LOVE and ELECTRIC LADYLAND?

8. Early on in Beatle days, John Lennon wrote his first book: what was it called?

9. TV's TOP OF THE POPS used to feature a girl playing the records: what was her name?

10. When Terry Sylvester joined the Hollies, who did he replace?

Mums and Dads

1. Complete this group's name: Frankie Lymon and . . . ?

2. For which curiously named group was TOM HARK a big hit in 1958?

3. By what name was American singer J. P. Richardson better known?

4. Which comedy actor made MAD PASSIONATE LOVE in 1958?

5. Who had hits with YAKETY YAK, CHARLIE BROWN and POISON IVY?

6. Was LOVE IS A MANY SPLENDOURED THING a hit for the Four Preps, the Four Aces or the Four Seasons?

7. Who tried a little FRIENDLY PERSUASION and then wrote LOVE LETTERS IN THE SAND?

8. Still around as an actor, he had a big hit with BE MY GIRL at the end of 1957: who is he? *Jim Dale*

9. For which American rock 'n' roll group was GIDDY UP A DING DONG a hit in 1956? *Freddie Bell & the Bell Boys.*

10. Who sang PASSING STRANGERS with Billy Eckstine?

Grandparents

1. In which film was the song WHITE CHRISTMAS first heard – and who wrote it?

2. What is the next line in this song: 'A you're adorable'?

3. Who played THE HARRY LIME THEME in the film THE THIRD MAN?

4. Who played the parts of Tweety Pie and Sylvester on I TAUT I TAW A PUDDY TAT?

5. Who supplied Rossano Brazzi's singing voice in the film SOUTH PACIFIC?

6. Who played the leading role in CALL ME MADAM on the screen?

7. Complete this song title: GILLY-GILLY-OSSEN-FEFFER . . .

8. Who is said to have the voice of the century?

9. Who called his orchestra the Royal Canadians?

10. In which film did Judy Garland sing THE TROLLEY SONG?

These cartoons represent a TV show of the early sixties and a West End stage musical of the early seventies. Name both.

Lyrics for eggheads

A final selection of lines from ten hit songs for you to identify adding, if you can, the name of the singer or group who first recorded the song.

1. 'Leave your books and get out in the sun, summer's here and we're gonna have fun'. _BCR's_

2. 'When I get older losing my hair'. _Beatles older I'm 64_

3. 'The old home town looks the same as I step down from the train'. _Green Green Grass of Home TJ._

4. 'Now since my baby left me I've found a new place to dwell'.

5. 'The movie's over, it's four o'clock and we're in trouble deep'.

6. 'Tonight's the night I've waited for, because you're not a baby any more'.

7. 'Imagine a still summer's day when nothing is moving – least of all me'.

8. 'I love the colourful clothes she wears, and the way the sunlight plays upon her hair'.

9. 'The Eastern world it is explodin', violence flarin' and bullets loadin'.'

10. 'You think we look pretty good together, you think my shoes are made of leather'. _Substitute - Who_

Remember when?

Another test for your memory: can you put a date against each of the following hit records?

1. HIGH IN THE SKY by Amen Corner

2. I CAN'T STOP LOVING YOU by Ray Charles

✓72 3. ROCKET MAN by Elton John

✓60 4. TELL LAURA I LOVE HER by Ricky Valance

5. (THERE'S) ALWAYS SOMETHING THERE TO REMIND ME by Sandie Shaw

6. IT'S SO EASY by Andy Williams

7. TAKE GOOD CARE OF MY BABY by Bobby Vee

S8 ̶6̶4̶ 8. ALL I HAVE TO DO IS DREAM by the Everly Brothers

6̶6̶ 9. YOU DON'T HAVE TO SAY YOU LOVE ME by Dusty Springfield

10. ALL BECAUSE OF YOU by Geordie

Jackpot Special

Radio 1 listeners who take part in POP THE QUESTION can, should they win five album tokens, choose to attempt a more difficult three-part Jackpot question which, if answered correctly, brings a substantial bonus prize. On the next four pages, we print a selection of these tricky posers: how do you shape up against the experts hanging on to the end of a telephone?

1. Here are lines from the lyrics of three Rolling Stones hits. Can you name the songs from which they come?
   (A) 'She would never say where she came from, yesterday don't matter if it's gone'.
   (B) 'I see the girls go by dressed in their summer clothes'.
   (C) 'Well it seems to me that you have seen too much in too few years and though you try you just can't hide your eyes against real tears'.

2. Listed below are three sets of song titles each of which has been taken from an LP by a well-known group. Can you name the group from the titles given?
   (A) POLYTHENE PAM, COME TOGETHER and SUN KING.
   (B) SO SAD ABOUT US, BORIS THE SPIDER and A QUICK ONE WHILE HE'S AWAY.
   (C) I'M WAITING FOR THE DAY, CAROLINE NO and WOULDN'T IT BE NICE.

3. This question concerns two British groups and one American one. From the three lists of personnel, can you identify the groups?
   (A) Chris Britton, Reg Presley, Ronnie Bond and Pete Staples.

    (B) Dennis Bryon, Clive Taylor, Andy Fairweather-Low, Alan Jones, Blue Weaver, Mike Smith and Neil Jones.

    (C) Mike Clark, Chris Hillman, Jim McGuinn, Gene Clark and Dave Crosby.

4. In the three sets of song titles given below, one word in each set which is common to those songs has been left out. Can you guess the word in each case?

    (A) ----'S JUST A BROKEN HEART, SECRET ----, and I ---- HOW YOU ---- ME.

    (B) ANYONE WHO HAD A -----, ----- OF STONE and -----BEAT.

    (C) ----- WITH ME, ----- WITH THE GUITAR MAN and ------ ON.

5. Some groups and duos are known by their surnames: do you know the Christian names of these three acts?

    (A) The Everly Brothers.

    (B) Crosby, Stills, Nash and Young.

    (C) Marvin, Welch and Farrar.

6. The three songs listed below were all revivals of earlier hits. Can you name the artists who originally had hits with the songs?

    (A) BREAKING UP IS HARD TO DO by the Partridge Family.

    (B) WHY by Donny Osmond.

    (C) COME SOFTLY TO ME by the New Seekers.

7. Take a look at the three groups of song titles here and see if you can decide who composed each group.

    (A) LOVELY RITA, DO YOU WANT TO KNOW A SECRET and IF I FELL. *Lennon/McCartney*

    (B) AS TEARS GO BY, RUBY TUESDAY and DANDELION.

    (C) SUNDAY AFTERNOON, DANDY and MR PLEASANT. *Ray Davies*

8. In the three lists of group members given below, one name is wrong. Do you know which is the wrong one and whose name should be there?
   (A) SLADE: Don Powell, Jimmy Lea, Eric Stewart and Noddy Holder.
   (B) THE MOODY BLUES: Graeme Edge, John Lodge, Mike Pinder, Jimmy Page and Ray Thomas.
   (C) THE HOLLIES: Tony Hicks, Bobby Elliott, Bern Calvert, Michael D'Abo and Terry Sylvester.

9. Read the three sentences given carefully and decide whether or not the statements are correct.
   (A) YOU DON'T HAVE TO SAY YOU LOVE ME, STEP INSIDE LOVE and IN THE MIDDLE OF NOWHERE were all hits for Dusty Springfield.
   (B) IT'S ALL OVER NOW, GET OFF MY CLOUD and NOT FADE AWAY were all hits for the Rolling Stones.
   (C) BABY LOVE, THE HAPPENING and DANCING IN THE STREET were all hits for the Supremes.

10. Try and put the three sets of hits listed into the order in which they were released.
    (A) The Beatles: GET BACK; PLEASE PLEASE ME; HELP.
    (B) Elvis Presley: GUITAR MAN; IT'S NOW OR NEVER; HEARTBREAK HOTEL.
    (C) Cliff Richard: MOVE IT; THE DAY I MET MARIE; BACHELOR BOY.

11. This is a question about brothers and sisters. Each of the well-known singers listed has either a brother or sister in the music business: can you name them?
    (A) Mick Jagger.
    (B) Dusty Springfield.
    (C) Dionne Warwick.

12. How well do you know your B sides? Each of the songs listed below has been on the flipside of a hit: can you identify the groups who recorded each group of songs?
    (A) PLAY WITH FIRE, THE SINGER NOT THE SONG and AS TEARS GO BY.
    (B) DOCTOR DOCTOR, INSTANT PARTY and THE OX.
    (C) YOU'RE SO GOOD TO ME, WENDY and THE WARMTH OF THE SUN.

13. Song-writers often work in well-established teams. The three names of composers given below are each half of such a team: can you name their partners?
    (A) Nicky Chinn.
    (B) Tony Hatch.
    (C) Gerry Goffin.

14. Some artists are described as 'one-hit wonders'. The groups and singer given here have each had only one Top 20 hit: what were their songs called?
    (A) The Johnny Mann Singers.
    (B) Thunderclap Newman.
    (C) Karen Young.

Top Five

One of the most popular features of Johnnie Walker's Radio 1 programme has been the weekly Top 5 when listeners are invited to vote for their favourite record by a particular singer or group. The next few pages are devoted to a list of the results of some of these polls, beginning in each case with the record that received the most votes. As a teaser, the names of the relevant artists are included with the other answers further on in the book.

1. THESE FOOLISH THINGS
   THE 'IN' CROWD   *B. Ferry*
   ANOTHER TIME, ANOTHER PLACE
   A HARD RAIN'S A-GONNA FALL
   SMOKE GETS IN YOUR EYES

2. O CAROL
   STANDING ON THE INSIDE
   GOING NOWHERE   *N. Sedaka*
   LAUGHTER IN THE RAIN
   OUR LAST SONG TOGETHER

3. MR TAMBOURINE MAN
   CHESTNUT MARE   *Byrds*
   I WASN'T BORN TO FOLLOW
   TURN TURN TURN
   YOU AIN'T GOIN' NOWHERE

4. VIRGINIA PLAIN
   DO THE STRAND
   A SONG FOR EUROPE
   PYJAMARAMA   *Roxy*
   MOTHER OF PEARL   *Music*

5. SPACE ODDITY •
   LIFE ON MARS   *D.B.*
   THE JEAN GENIE
   ROCK 'N' ROLL SUICIDE
   THE PRETTIEST STAR

6. MAGGIE MAY •
   MANDOLIN WIND   *R.S.*
   TWISTING THE NIGHT AWAY
   REASON TO BELIEVE
   YOU WEAR IT WELL

7. COZ I LUV YOU
   DARLING BE HOME SOON
   CUM ON FEEL THE NOIZE   *S*
   MAMA WEER ALL CRAZEE NOW
   TAKE ME BACK 'OME

8. HONKY TONK WOMEN
   (I CAN'T GET NO) SATISFACTION
   BROWN SUGAR
   RUBY TUESDAY   *Stones*
   ANGIE •

114

9. HEY JUDE
   YESTERDAY *   *Beatles*
   LET IT BE
   STRAWBERRY FIELDS FOREVER
   ELEANOR RIGBY

10. GOD ONLY KNOWS
    GOOD VIBRATIONS   *B. B.*
    DARLIN'
    SLOOP JOHN B
    I GET AROUND

11. YOUR SONG *
    ROCKET MAN   *E. J*
    CROCODILE ROCK
    DANIEL
    GOODBYE YELLOW BRICK ROAD

12. BRIDGE OVER TROUBLED WATER
    SOUNDS OF SILENCE **
    THE BOXER   *S & g*
    I AM A ROCK
    HOMEWARD BOUND

13. IT'S NOW OR NEVER
    JAILHOUSE ROCK
    WOODEN HEART   *EP.*
    RETURN TO SENDER *
    ALL SHOOK UP

14. HOW CAN I TELL YOU
    MORNING HAS BROKEN
    BOY WITH A MOON AND STAR ON HIS HEAD
    MOONSHADOW
    FATHER AND SON *C. S.*

15. GREAT BALLS OF FIRE *Jerry*
    JAMBALAYA *Lee Lewis*
    WHOLE LOTTA SHAKIN' GOIN' ON
    JOHNNY B. GOODE
    GOOD GOLLY MISS MOLLY

16. LIVING DOLL
    VISIONS *C. Richard*
    THE DAY I MET MARIE
    THE MINUTE YOU'RE GONE
    THE YOUNG ONES

17. BABY LOVE
    STOP! IN THE NAME OF LOVE
    SOMEDAY WE'LL BE TOGETHER
    YOU CAN'T HURRY LOVE
    FLOY JOY

18. NIGHTS IN WHITE SATIN
    GO NOW! *Moody*
    QUESTION *Blues*
    I'M JUST A SINGER (IN A ROCK AND ROLL BAND)
    RIDE MY SEE-SAW

19. HE AIN'T HEAVY ... HE'S MY BROTHER
    STOP STOP STOP
    LONG COOL WOMAN IN A BLACK DRESS
    BUS STOP
    STAY   *Hollies*

20. REACH OUT, I'LL BE THERE
    WALK AWAY RENEE
    I CAN'T HELP MYSELF
    STILL WATER
    DO WHAT YOU'VE GOTTA DO

21. ALONE AGAIN (NATURALLY)
    CLAIR
    NOTHING RHYMED   *g.o's*
    MATRIMONY
    GET DOWN

22. PINBALL WIZARD
    WON'T GET FOOLED AGAIN
    THE MAGIC BUS
    SUBSTITUTE   *who*
    MY GENERATION

23. LET ME IN
    THAT'S MY GIRL
    CRAZY HORSES   *O*
    DOWN BY THE LAZY RIVER
    DARLIN'

117

24. LAY LADY LAY
    JUST LIKE A WOMAN
    LIKE A ROLLING STONE
    POSITIVELY 4TH STREET
    MR TAMBOURINE MAN

25. YOU ARE THE SUNSHINE OF MY LIFE
    MY CHERIE AMOUR
    SUPERSTITION
    FOR ONCE IN MY LIFE
    I WAS MADE TO LOVE HER

26. EBONY EYES
    ALL I HAVE TO DO IS DREAM
    CATHY'S CLOWN
    BYE BYE LOVE
    CRYING IN THE RAIN

27. I'LL BE THERE
    I WANT YOU BACK
    DOCTOR MY EYES
    LOOKIN' THROUGH THE WINDOWS
    SKYWRITER

28. IT DOESN'T MATTER ANYMORE
    TRUE LOVE WAYS
    PEGGY SUE
    THAT'LL BE THE DAY
    EVERYDAY

118

29. HOT LOVE

    RIDE A WHITE SWAN

    METAL GURU

    GET IT ON

    JEEPSTER

T. Resc.

30. MONEY

    TIME

    BRAIN DAMAGE

    US AND THEM

    THE GREAT GIG IN THE SKY

Pink Floyd

WE CAN WORK IT OUT . . . CAN YOU?

As a parting shot, see how many words of three letters or more
you can find in the letters that make up POP THE QUES-
TION. Avoid place names, proper names, plurals, abbrevi-
ations, prefixes and suffixes – and use the letters only once,
which means no words with two Ns, for example. We've
checked our list against the Concise Oxford Dictionary. See
how you get on!
RATINGS: 50 – DIM; 100 – AVERAGE; 150 – GROOVY;
200 – RIGHT ON!; 250+ – FANTASTIC!!

ANSWERS

8. The Partridge Family.   9. The Peppers.   10. Peters and Lee

20   1. The Carpenters   2. Chicory Tip   3. Christie   4. Incidentally   5. Dave and Ansel Collins   6. Brian Connolly   7. Terry Dactyl and the Dinosaurs   8. Roger Daltrey   9. LADY D'ARBANVILLE   10. Neil Diamond

21   1. Herb Alpert   2. Roy C   3. Johnny Cash   4. Joe Cocker   5. COLD TURKEY   6. Crosby Stills and Nash   7. Desmond Dekker and the Aces   8. Guitar   9. EDELWEISS   10. Emerson Lake and Palmer

22   1. Bobby Darin   2. BOBBY'S GIRL   3. Georgie Fame   4. The Fortunes   5. Connie Francis   6. Alan Freeman   7. Bill Haley and the Comets   8. HAVE I THE RIGHT   9. HOOTS MON   10. David Jacobs

23   1. Ivor Novello   2. Shirley Temple   3. Lonnie Donegan   4. Johnnie Ray   5. Bobbysoxers   6. Ginger Rogers   7. Parlophone   8. Jack Payne   9. The Ink Spots   10. Piano

24   MY GUY; ROCKIN ROBIN

25   1. Year   2. Iceland   3. Stardust   4. Chart   5. Ire   6. Alan   7. Disc   8. Veal   9. Dodd   10. Army   11. Sun   12. Dusty   The American singer: David Cassidy

26   1. LET ME IN (The Osmonds)   2. LONG HAIRED LOVER FROM LIVERPOOL (Jimmy Osmond)   3. MERRY CHRISTMAS EVERYBODY (Slade)   4. MINUETTO ALLEGRETTO (The Wombles)   5. SCHOOL LOVE (Barry Blue)   6. THE STREAK (Ray Stevens)   7. TWO LITTLE BOYS (Rolf Harris)   8. AND I LOVE YOU SO (Perry Como)   9. BALL-ROOM BLITZ (Sweet)   10. BIG YELLOW TAXI (Joni Mitchell)

27   1. The Osmonds   2. Suzi Quatro   3. The Rubettes   4. SAD SWEET DREAMER   5. Sparks   6. STOP STOP STOP (!)   7. Twenty (!!)   8. The Wombles   9. Abba   10. Clive Dunn

28   1. Tony Christie   2. Alice Cooper   3. Sacha Distel

4. LOVE GROWS (WHERE MY ROSEMARY GOES)   5. Electric Light Orchestra   6. David Essex   7. Fluff   8. 48 CRASH   9. Free   10. Art Garfunkel

29   1. The Equals   2. EVE OF DESTRUCTION   3. EVERLASTING LOVE   4. Marianne Faithfull   5. Marvin Gaye   6. THE GOOD, THE BAD AND THE UGLY   7. HAIR   8. HANG ON SLOOPY   9. A HARD DAY'S NIGHT   10. True

30   1. Perry Como   2. Piano   3. The Four Seasons   4. Gerry and the Pacemakers   5. I'LL NEVER FIND ANOTHER YOU   6. Eden Kane   7. MY GUY   8. Jim Reeves   9. P. J. Proby   10. Buddy Holly

31   1. Vera Lynn   2. His Master's Voice   3. Cinema organ   4. Siegfried   5. The Mills Brothers   6. 42ND STREET   7. STARS FELL ON ALABAMA   8. Richard   9. Phil Harris   10. Mary Ford

32   FOOL ON THE HILL; HELTER SKELTER

33

```
J   O   H   N   N   R   L   A   W   O   J
O   H   O   J   R   E   K   I   E   H   O
K   I   H   W   N   H   O   N   N   H   H
I   N   N   K   N   W   J   R   E   O   J
E   W   A   E   I   E   O   E   H   E   R
W   K   L   W   K   ■   R   K   E   K   L
R   E   R   A   L   K   E   L   E   E   A
J   O   H   I   E   E   L   A   I   E   W
H   R   N   N   W   I   E   W   N   N   H
O   H   W   L   A   N   N   H   I   N   O
J   O   H   K   E   R   J   O   H   O   J
```

◄ ⁄⁄⁄ Start here

Page

34 1. ROSE GARDEN   2. Sweet Sensation   3. Gary Glitter   4. Johnnie Walker   5. Gilbert O'Sullivan 6. The Who   7. GOOD VIBRATIONS   8. Bryan Ferry   9. Stevie Wonder   10. SPANISH FLEA

35 1. Steve Harley and Cockney Rebel   2. JANUARY 3. Mac and Katie Kissoon   4. MORNING SIDE OF THE MOUNTAIN   5. YOU YOU YOU   6. Queen 7. The Wombles   8. Hello   9. GET DANCING 10. 247 metres

36 1. GIMME DAT DING   2. GOOD GRIEF CHRISTINA   3. Isaac Hayes   4. Brother   5. Jimmy Helms   6. Herman   7. HI HO SILVER LINING   8. Mary Hopkin   9. Elton John   10. T. Rex

37 1. THOSE WERE THE DAYS   2. I WAS KAISER BILL'S BATMAN   3. Roger Miller   4. Tom Jones 5. EXCERPT FROM 'A TEENAGE OPERA'   6. Phil Spector   7. THE LAST WALTZ   8. Noel Harrison   9. OH WELL was a hit for Fleetwood Mac 10. PUPPET ON A STRING

38 1. Helen Shapiro   2. Don and Phil   3. IT'S NOT UNUSUAL   4. Debbie Reynolds   5. Jimmy Rodgers 6. A PUB WITH NO BEER   7. Fats Domino   8. Jerry Keller   9. Guy Mitchell   10. Soeur Sourire, the Singing Nun

39 1. WIZARD OF OZ   2. Teresa Brewer   3. I'D HAVE BAKED A CAKE   4. RUDOLPH THE RED-NOSED REINDEER   5. Guy Mitchell   6. MOONLIGHT SERENADE   7. Eve Boswell   8. Allan Jones   9. Duke Ellington   10. Mel Torme

40 The Bee Gees; Canned Heat; Gun; The Ink Spots

41 1. BILLY DON'T BE A HERO (Paper Lace)   2. CANDLE IN THE WIND (Elton John)   3. DAY DREAMER (David Cassidy)   4. YOU'RE SIXTEEN (Ringo Starr/Johnnie Burnette)   5. KUNG FU FIGHTING (Carl Douglas)   6. GONNA MAKE YOU A STAR (David Essex)   7. I SHOT THE SHERIFF (Eric Clapton)   8. ANNIE'S SONG (John

Denver)   9. I WISH IT COULD BE CHRISTMAS
EVERY DAY (Wizzard)   10. MY FRIEND STAN
(Slade)

42   Code 1: 1. TIE A YELLOW RIBBON   2. HORSE
WITH NO NAME   3. BACK STABBERS   4.
SEASONS IN THE SUN   5. KING OF THE
ROAD   Code 2: 1. GET OFF OF MY CLOUD   2.
MY NAME IS JACK   3. TIME IS TIGHT   4.
THOSE WERE THE DAYS   5. A WHITER
SHADE OF PALE

43   1. Jimmy   2. Wizzard   3. AMAZING GRACE was a
hit for the Royal Scots Dragoon Guards.   4. Charles
Aznavour   5. Barry Blue.   6. Slade   7. IF   8.
Jackson 5   9. Rolf Harris   10. Sweet

44   1. ALBATROSS   2. True   3. Bobby Bloom   4.
David Bowie   5. Brother and sister   6. Cockney Rebel
7. Les Crane   8. GAYE   9. Mick Jagger   10. John
Kongos

45   1. False   2. BABY PLEASE DON'T GO or HERE
COMES THE NIGHT.   3. The Bee Gees   4.
Martha Reeves and the Vandellas   5. HOLD TIGHT
6. Doors   7. David Gates   8. Honeybus   9. IN THE
YEAR 2525   10. MAGICAL MYSTERY TOUR

46   1. The Allisons   2. Brian Epstein   3. Little Richard
4. The Four Pennies   5. The Shadows   6. DON'T
LET THE SUN CATCH YOU CRYING/TO
KNOW YOU IS TO LOVE YOU/WHEN YOU
WALK IN THE ROOM   7. YOU REALLY GOT
ME   8. Ken Dodd   9. 1963   10. Pat Boone

47   1. And his Band of Renown   2. LAND OF SMILES
3. Henry Hall   4. Harp; Flies; Sweetest   5. Eric
Coates   6. Richard Tauber   7. Walter   8. Norman
Wisdom   9. Eddie Calvert   10. Anne Shelton

A(1)		G(2)		K(3)				N(4)		T(5)		B(6)
M		A(7)	M	E	N		C(8)	A	S	H		R
A		N		I		A(9)		I		E		A
N(10)	I	G	H	T				R(11)	O	B	I	N
D				H		M		O		A		D
A(12)	B(13)	B	A		J(14)	A	N	B	E	R	R	Y
		A		U(15)		C		I		O		
R(16)	O	B	I	N	S	O	N		O(17)	N	C	E(18)
O		Y		R		G		R(19)		E		V
W(20)	I	L	D	E				A(21)	L	F(22)	I	E
L		O		A		N		D		I		R
E		V(23)	A	D	O			C(24)	A	R	R	L
S		E		Y				R		E		Y

50   KING OF THE ROAD; GET OFF OF MY CLOUD

51   1. The Osmonds   2. Dave Lee Travis   3. Bobby 'Boris' Pickett and the Crypt Kickers   4. Stephanie de Sykes   5. Lynsey de Paul   6. MOULDY OLD DOUGH was a hit for Lieutenant Pigeon   7. MORNINGTOWN RIDE   8. Piano   9. EYE LEVEL 10. Barry White

52   1. Mungo Jerry   2. Wolfgang Amadeus Mozart   3. RUBY TUESDAY   4. Carly Simon   5. Cat Stevens   6. Shirley Jones   7. I WANT YOU BACK   8. POPCORN by Hot Butter   9. GHETTO CHILD   10. BRIDGET THE MIDGET

53   1. Nicky Chinn and Mike Chapman   2. Cupid's Inspiration   3. CATCH THE WIND   4. The Animals   5. Bobby Hebb   6. Steve Ellis   7. THE GRADUATE   8. Jimmy   9. LILY THE PINK   10. Brian Matthew

54 1. Freddie and the Dreamers   2. Lesley Gore   3.
ANYONE WHO HAD A HEART   4. BLOWING
IN THE WIND   5. Wayne Fontana and the Mind-
benders   6. Keith Fordyce   7. The Jordanaires   8.
Cliff Richard   9. JUST LIKE EDDIE   10. ELU-
SIVE BUTTERFLY

55 1. Victor Silvester   2. OKLAHOMA!   3. Ray Noble
4. Mandy Miller   5. ANNIE GET YOUR GUN   6.
Dame Cicely Courtneidge   7. Jimmy Dorsey   8.
SKYLINER   9. Piano   10. Bunny Berigan

56 YOU REALLY GOT A HOLD ON ME; YOU KEEP
ME HANGIN' ON

57 1. THE AIR THAT I BREATHE   2. ALL I HAVE
TO DO IS DREAM   3. Edison Lighthouse   4.
Emperor Rosko   5. Bay City Rollers   6. DANCING
ON A SATURDAY NIGHT   7. Emerson Lake and
Palmer   8. EVERYTHING IS BEAUTIFUL   9.
Fairport Convention   10. David Hamilton

58
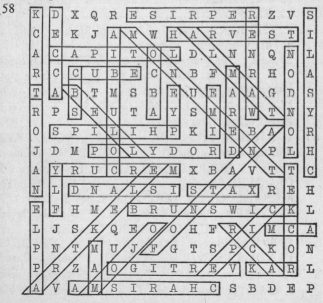

Page

128

Yoko Ono); C and Y (Sonny and Cher)   p.4: Dusty Springfield (The Springfields)   p.5: Don Powell (Slade)   p.6: Pete Townshend (The Who)   p.7: A – bass guitar (Suzi Quatro); B – lead guitar (Jimi Hendrix); C – banjo or guitar (Lonnie Donegan)   p.8: Alvin Stardust used to record as Shane Fenton and his real name is is Bernard Jewry   p.9: Gary Glitter used to record as Paul Raven and his read name is Paul Gadd   p.10: A – Mike McGear (brother of Paul McCartney); B – Derek Longmuir (brother of Alan, both in the Bay City Rollers); C – Don Everley (brother of Phil)   p.11: A – Rolling Stones (Brian Jones: he left group before he died); B – Manfred Mann (Paul Jones); C – Animals (Eric Burdon)   p.12: Carol, wife of the Tremeloes' Chip Hawkes (Chip is on p.13)   p.13: Leba, wife of Neil Sedaka (Neil is on p.16)   p.14: Molly, wife of Barry Gibb (Barry is on p.15)   p.15: Pauline, wife of the Sweet's Mick Tucker (Mick is on p.12)   p.16: Louise, wife of Slade's Jimmy Lea (Jimmy is on p.14)

67   1. DANCE WITH THE DEVIL   2. Mott the Hoople   3. Lee Marvin   4. Gilbert O'Sullivan   5. COULD IT BE I'M FALLING IN LOVE   6. Andy Kim   7. Liverpool   8. LOOP DI LOVE   9. Johnny Nash   10. PLEASE TELL HIM THAT I SAID HELLO/ GOOD LOVE CAN NEVER DIE/THE SECRETS THAT YOU KEEP

68   1. America   2. Bryan Ferry   3. Samantha   4. Lobo   5. 1967   6. SULTANA was a hit for Titanic   7. Kenny   8. British Broadcasting Corporation   9. The Chiffons   10. GROOVIN' WITH MR BLOE

69   1. Edwin Hawkins Singers   2. Herman's Hermits   3. Ireland   4. LADY GODIVA   5. MONDAY MONDAY   6. False. He had a hit with JENNIFER JUNIPER   7. The Kinks   8. Lulu   9. Pink Floyd   10. The Troggs

70   1. The Everly Brothers   2. The Barron Knights   3. LOVE ME DO   4. RHYTHM OF THE RAIN   5. Frankie Vaughan   6. THANK YOUR LUCKY

STARS   7. Richard Starkey   8. Cliff Richard   9. JUKE BOX JURY   10. I LOVE MY DOG

71   1. Al Bowlly   2. Springtime; Baby; Waterfront   3. Jessie Matthews   4. Stan Kenton   5. Rosemary Clooney   6. Doris Day   7. Gracie Fields   8. Carmen Miranda   9. Joe Loss   10. Patti, Maxine and Laverne

72   CRYING IN THE CHAPEL; MR TAMBOURINE MAN

73   1. EASY BEAT   2. Nashville   3. Honeycombs   4. Overlanders   5. Nelson   6. Equals   7. Price   8. Temptations   9. Wonder   10. Searchers   11. Eddy   12. Donovan   13. Tornados   The pop musician is Pete Townshend

74   1. 1969   2. 1973   3. 1959   4. 1965   5. 1971   6. 1961   7. 1964   8. 1970   9. 1963   10. 1967

75   1. Arsenal First Team Squad   2. Peter Skellern   3. Archie Bell and the Drells   4. The Three Degrees   5. PAPER ROSES   6. Michael Jackson   7. Cilla Black   8. Scaffold   9. Hotlegs   10. Keith Moon

76   1. ALSO SPRACH ZARATHUSTRA, Opus 30   2. Colin Blunstone   3. Detroit   4. Adam Faith   5. His Master's Voice   6. Carole King   7. New York City   8. Tim Rice and Andrew Lloyd-Webber   9. SERGEANT PEPPER'S LONELY HEARTS CLUB BAND   10. RAINDROPS KEEP FALLING ON MY HEAD

77   1. Abraham Lincoln, Martin Luther King and John F. Kennedy   2. The Bedrocks   3. CATCH US IF YOU CAN   4. Leitch   5. Sam Cooke   6. Val Doonican   7. Bob Dylan   8. Chris Farlowe   9. Genesis   10. The Honeycombs

78   1. ALL DAY AND ALL OF THE NIGHT   2. BRING IT ON HOME TO ME/I WOULDN'T TRADE YOU FOR THE WORLD/AS LONG AS HE NEEDS ME   3. The Searchers   4. Col. Tom Parker   5. Joe Meek   6. Thomas Hicks   7. The Cavern Club   8. Peter Asher   9. FROM A JACK TO A KING   10. The Applejacks

130

79 1. Trombone   2. Leslie Sarony   3. B. C. Hilliam and Malcolm McEachern   4. Sir Alan Herbert   5. DANGEROUS MOONLIGHT   6. Reg Dixon   7. Harry Gold   8. BRIGADOON   9. Chick Webb 10. Kay Kyser

80 DRIVE MY CAR; MICHAEL (ROW THE BOAT ASHORE)

81 LETTER CODE: To break this, reverse the alphabet so that A = Z and Z = A. Then add further lines alongside, moving each line up one letter so that A progressively equals Z, Y, X and W. When coding, use Z for the first A, Y for the second and so on. The answers are: 1. Harold Melvin and the Blue Notes   2. Smokey Robinson and the Miracles   3. Billy J. Kramer and the Dakotas   4. The Four Seasons   5. Brotherhood of Man

NUMBER CODE: Number the alphabet from 1 to 26 then reverse these numbers so that A = 26 and Z = 1. Add 100 to each number, so that A = 126, then simply turn each number round which makes A = 621. The answers are: 1. THEIR SATANIC MAJESTIES REQUEST (Rolling Stones)   2. AXIS BOLD AS LOVE (Jimi Hendrix)   3. ALL THINGS MUST PASS (George Harrison)   4. DARK SIDE OF THE MOON (Pink Floyd)   5. CRIME OF THE CENTURY (Supertramp)

82 1. HEY GIRL DON'T BOTHER ME   2. The Isley Brothers   3. Noel Edmonds   4. ROCK AND ROLL WINTER   5. BREAKING DOWN THE WALLS OF HEARTACHE   6. Creedence Clearwater Revival 7. DON'T FORGET TO REMEMBER   8. THE LEGEND OF XANADU   9. Alan Freeman   10. Cat Stevens

83 HEY ROCK AND ROLL   2. Terry Jacks   3. The Mixtures   4. Mungo Jerry   5. Nazareth   6. The New Seekers   7. THE LAST TIME: the others are all Beatles songs   8. Diana Ross   9. Stealers Wheel 10. Argent

84 1. The Band   2. Mike Batt   3. Clarence Carter   4. Three   5. I DIDN'T KNOW I LOVED YOU ('TIL I SAW YOU ROCK AND ROLL)   6. Jermaine Jackson   7. Vicky Leandros   8. Marilyn Monroe   9. Mud   10. Michael Pasternak

85 1. Mothers of Invention   2. Love Sculpture   3. Arlo Guthrie   4. JE T'AIME MOI NON PLUS   5. John Lennon   6. I CAN'T EXPLAIN   7. Anita Harris   8. GIMME LITTLE SIGN   9. FLOWERS IN THE RAIN by the Move   10. DON'T BRING ME YOUR HEARTACHES

86 1. Cliff Bennett   2. BLUE CHRISTMAS   3. Billy Fury   4. Jet Harris   5. I WANNA BE YOUR MAN   6. Jack Good   7. KIMBERLEY JIM   8. Eamonn Andrews   9. Winifred Atwell   10. PETITE FLEUR

87 1. Hubert Gregg   2. GUYS AND DOLLS   3. Sammy Kaye   4. His Rippling Rhythm Orchestra   5. Vibraphone   6. Edward Kennedy Ellington   7. Five   8. BLUE SKIES   9. Miss Otis   10. WHERE THE BLUE OF THE NIGHT

88 JAILHOUSE ROCK; BEGGAR'S BANQUET

89 1. BLUE SUEDE SHOES (Elvis Presley/Carl Perkins)   2. IT MIGHT AS WELL RAIN UNTIL SEPTEMBER (Carole King)   3. AQUARIUS (Fifth Dimension)   4. DELILAH (Tom Jones)   5. ELEANOR RIGBY (The Beatles)   6. LEADER OF THE PACK (The Shangri-las)   7. GOD ONLY KNOWS (The Beach Boys)   8. RIVER DEEP – MOUNTAIN HIGH (Ike and Tina Turner)   9. SPACE ODDITY (David Bowie)   10. THIS FLIGHT TONIGHT (Nazareth)

90 1. Treacle   2. Hindus   3. Emitted   4. Breaks   5. Earning   6. Armoury   7. Tie; Via   8. Low; Oaf   9. Earnest   10. Sprain   The quotation is: 'Picture yourself in a boat on a river with tangerine trees and marmalade skies' from LUCY IN THE SKY WITH DIAMONDS by the Beatles

93 1. MOTHER OF MINE   2. Don McLean   3. Rod Stewart   4. Ashton, Gardner and Dyke   5. C.C.S.

6. Charlie Rich 7. Hawkwind 8. JEALOUS MIND
9. Tami Lyn 10. Queen

94 1. Arrows 2. Delaney and Bonnie and Friends 3.
The New Seekers 4. Scott English 5. The EXOR-
CIST 6. Radha Krishna Temple 7. Noddy Holder
and Jimmy Lea 8. Dandy Livingstone 9. PIN-
BALL WIZARD 10. Sakkarin

95 1. AIN'T NOTHING BUT A HOUSE-PARTY 2.
The Bachelors 3. June Carter 4. Eric Clapton 5.
DIZZY: the others are all instrumentals 6. Gerry
Dorsey 7. EVERYBODY'S TALKIN' 8. CORO-
NATION STREET 9. GO NOW! 10. HELP!

96 1. The Avons or Paul Evans and the Curls or the Lana
Sisters or Garry Mills 2. Paul Anka 3. Richie
Valens and the Big Bopper 4. Pearl Carr and Teddy
Johnson 5. The Champs 6. Doris Day 7. Pounds;
Smiling; Blue 8. Charlie Drake 9. The Kalin Twins
10. Tupelo, Mississippi

97 1. THE BLUE ANGEL 2. Frances Gumm 3.
Jimmy Kennedy 4. Larry Parks 5. TONIGHT
6. Lale Anderson 7. Tony Martin 8. PERCHANCE
TO DREAM 9. THREE LITTLE PIGS 10. Alice
Faye

98 ROLL OVER BEETHOVEN; I'M LOOKING
THROUGH YOU

99 1. Elvis Presley 2. THE OTHER MAN'S GRASS
3. The Beach Boys 4. NIGHTS IN WHITE SATIN
5. GONNA MAKE YOU AN OFFER YOU CAN'T
REFUSE 6. The Spencer Davis Group 7. DEDI-
CATED FOLLOWER OF FASHION 8. BEND
ME SHAPE ME 9. CAST YOUR FATE TO THE
WIND 10. Tony Blackburn

100 1. Satisfaction 2. Casuals 3. Pilot 4. Lennon 5.
Holly 6. Puppet 7. Imagine 8. Everlasting 9.
Tommy 10. Righteous 11. Orbison The pop per-
sonality: Phil Spector

101 1. Smokey Robinson and the Miracles 2. Roxy Music
3. Blackfoot Sue 4. George Harrison 5. The Piglets

133

6. The Rolling Stones   7. New World   8. Julio; Smile; Strawberry   9. Paul McCartney   10. Jones

102   1. Shirley Bassey   2. Horace Faith   3. Golden Earring   4. Alex Hughes   5. LOVE OF THE COMMON PEOPLE   6. Melanie Safka   7. Alan Price   8. Diana Ross, Supremes and Temptations   9. Ed Stewart   10. Juicy Lucy

103   1. Guitar   2. Ginger Baker   3. THE CLAPPING SONG   4. Chris Denning   5. Judith Durham   6. FINCHLEY CENTRAL   7. Jimi Hendrix   8. IN HIS OWN WRITE   9. Samantha Juste   10. Graham Nash

104   1. The Teenagers   2. Elias and his Zig Zag Jive Flutes   3. Big Bopper   4. Bernard Bresslaw   5. The Coasters   6. Four Aces   7. Pat Boone   8. Jim Dale   9. Freddie Bell and the Bell Boys   10. Sarah Vaughan

105   1. HOLIDAY INN; Irving Berlin   2. 'B you're so beautiful'   3. Anton Karas   4. Mel Blanc   5. Giorgio Tozzi   6. Ethel Merman   7. KATZENELLEN-BOGEN-BY-THE-SEA   8. Sarah Vaughan   9. Guy Lombardo   10. MEET ME IN ST LOUIS

106   COOL FOR CATS; THE ROCKY HORROR SHOW

107   1. SUMMERLOVE SENSATION (Bay City Rollers)   2. WHEN I'M SIXTY-FOUR (The Beatles)   3. GREEN GREEN GRASS OF HOME (Tom Jones)   4. HEARTBREAK HOTEL (Elvis Presley)   5. WAKE UP LITTLE SUSIE (The Everly Brothers)   6. HAPPY BIRTHDAY SWEET SIXTEEN (Neil Sedaka)   7. THE DAY I MET MARIE (Cliff Richard)   8. GOOD VIBRATIONS (The Beach Boys)   9. EVE OF DESTRUCTION (Barry McGuire)   10. SUBSTITUTE (The Who)

108   1. 1968   2. 1962   3. 1972   4. 1960   5. 1964   6. 1970   7. 1961   8. 1958   9. 1966   10. 1973

109   1. (A) RUBY TUESDAY (B) PAINT IT, BLACK (C) 19TH NERVOUS BREAKDOWN   2. (A) The Beatles (B) The Who (C) The Beach Boys   3. (A) The Troggs (B) Amen Corner (C) The Byrds

Page
110 4. (A) Love (B) Heart (C) Dance   5. (A) Don and Phil
(B) Dave, Stephen, Graham and Neil (C) Hank, Bruce
and John   6. (A) Neil Sedaka (B) Anthony Newley
(C) The Fleetwoods   7. (A) John Lennon and Paul
McCartney (B) Mick Jagger and Keith Richard (C) Ray
Davies

111 8. (A) Eric Stewart should be Dave Hill (B) Jimmy Page
should be Justin Hayward (C) Michael D'Abo should be
Allan Clarke   9. (A) STEP INSIDE LOVE was a hit
for Cilla Black (B) All correct (C) DANCING IN THE
STREET was a hit for Martha Reeves and the Vandellas
10. (A) PLEASE PLEASE ME, HELP, GET BACK
(B) HEARTBREAK HOTEL, IT'S NOW OR
NEVER, GUITAR MAN (C) MOVE IT, BACHELOR
BOY, THE DAY I MET MARIE   11. (A) Chris
Jagger (B) Tom Springfield (C) Dee Dee Warwick

112 12. (A) The Rolling Stones (B) The Who (C) The Beach
Boys   13. (A) Mike Chapman (B) Jackie Trent (C)
Carole King   14. (A) UP UP AND AWAY (B)
SOMETHING IN THE AIR (C) NOBODY'S CHILD

113 1. Bryan Ferry   2. Neil Sedaka   3. The Byrds

114 4. Roxy Music   5. David Bowie   6. Rod Stewart
7. Slade   8. The Rolling Stones

115 9. The Beatles   10. The Beach Boys   11. Elton John
12. Simon and Garfunkel   13. Elvis Presley

116 14. Cat Stevens   15. Jerry Lee Lewis   16. Cliff
Richard   17. The Supremes   18. The Moody Blues

117 19. The Hollies   20. The Four Tops   21. Gilbert
O'Sullivan   22. The Who   23. The Osmonds

118 24. Bob Dylan   25. Stevie Wonder   26. The Everly
Brothers   27. Jackson 5   28. Buddy Holly

119 29. T. Rex   30. Pink Floyd

119 Enthuse; epithet; epos; equine; equip; ethos; heinous;
hen; hep; het; hie; hint; hip; hipe; hippo; his; hist; hit;
hoe; hoist; hone; honest; hoop; hoot; hop; hope; hose;
host; hot; house; hue; hunt; hut; inquest; inset; instep;
into; ion; isotope; nest; net; nip; nit; noise; noisette;
noose; nose; not; note; nous; nut; one; onset; onto;

onus; open; ophite; opine; oppose; opposite; opt; option; opus; otiose; oust; out; peen; peep; pen; pent; penthouse; peon; pepsin; peptone; peso; pest; pet; petuntse; phone; phonetist; photo; phut; pie; pin; pine; pint; pinto; pious; pip; pipe; pipette; pique; piquet; pish; piston; pit; pith; poet; point; poise; poison; pooh; poop; pope; popish; pose; post; postpone; pot; poteen; potent; potion; pout; pun; punish; punt; pup; pus; push; put; putt; puttee; quest; quiet; quieten; quins; quint; quintet; quip; quit; quite; quits; quoin; quoit; quote; quoth; quotient; see; seen; seep; seine; sent; sept; sequin; set; seton; sett; she; sheen; sheep; sheet; shin; shine; ship; shoe; shone; shoo; shoot; shop; shot; shout; shun; shunt; shut; sin; sine; sip; siphon; siphonet; sippet; sit; site; snip; snippet; snoop; snot; snout; son; soon; soot; sooth; soothe; sop; sot; soup; south; spent; spin; spine; spinet; spit; spite; spittoon; spoon; spot; spout; spun; squint; squit; steep; step; steppe; stint; stone; stoop; stop; stout; stun; stunt; sue; suet; suit; suite; sun; sup; supine; suttee; ten; tenet; tense; tent; test; thee; then; thin; thine; this; those; thou; tie; tin; tine; tint; tip; tippet; tit; tithe; toe; ton; tone; too; toot; tooth; top; tope; topee; toupee; tout; tun; tune; tup; tut; unit; unite; unto; upon; uppish; upset; upshot.

Publishers for songs used in lyrics questions

Page 26
1. Intersong
2. E. H. Morris
3. Barn Publishing
4. Batt Songs
5. ATV Music
6. Peter Maurice/KPM
7. Herman Darewski
8. United Artists
9. Chinnichap/Rak
10. Siquomb

Page 66
1. Warner Bros
2. Rock Artists
3. Hawkana
4. Screen Gems/Columbia
5. Wizard Artists
6. Mustard
7. Big Ben
8. Essex
9. Blanedell
10. Chappell

Page 107
1. Martin-Coulter
2. Northern Songs
3. Burlington
4. Wood
5. Acuff-Rose

Page 41
1. Intune
2. Dick James
3. Palace
4. Jewel
5. Subiddu/Chappell
6. April/Rock On
7. Tuff Gong
8. ATV Music
9. Roy Wood/Carlin
10. Barn Publishing

Page 89
1. Aberbach
2. Dimension
3. United Artists
4. Donna
5. Northern Songs
6. Belinda
7. Immediate
8. Leiber Stoller
9. Essex
10. Joni Mitchell

6. Screen Gems/Columbia
7. Shadows
8. Immediate
9. Dick James
10. Fabulous

Rock on with Everest

HOW THE PLANETS RULE THE SUPERSTARS

Robert Leach 45p

Astrologer Robert Leach collects birthdays.

He has more than 4,000 in a vast filing system at his London home.

Among them is the horoscope of YOUR favourite superstar.

In his new book he reveals how the lives of pop stars are ruled by the signs of the Zodiac.

He tells:

WHY the Bay City Rollers are such a good team;

HOW Lulu's marriage broke up;

WHERE Mary Hopkin's career went wrong;

WHAT makes Jimmy Savile tick;

WHEN Slade will split up.

All the best-kept secrets of the pop world are revealed in this fascinating and sensational book.

Use the special order form at the end of this book

THE BAY CITY ROLLERS
OFFICIAL BIOGRAPHY

THIS IS THE STORY of a man and five boys.

The boys had the music and the man had the faith.

The boys: five teenagers from Edinburgh who left school and called themselves the Bay City Rollers.

The man: one-time Palais de Danse singer and potato lorry driver Tam Paton, who believed the boys would one day become Britain's top group.

His dream came true – but not before he and the Rollers had been through heartbreak and near-bankruptcy.

And when they started winning his troubles increased as rival pop moguls tried to take the group away from him.

As well as Tam Paton's highly personal and colourful story there are poignant contributions from Alan, Derek, Eric, Leslie and Woody.

Pages of never-seen-before photographs make this book a must for all Rollers fans.

And it is a fascinating story for anyone who has ever wondered why some groups succeed and others fail; for Tam Paton tells not only of his group's success but also how the pounds and pennies of the star system operate.

THE BAY CITY ROLLERS Michael Wale 45p

Use the special order form at the end of this book.

Coming soon

SO YOU WANT TO BE
IN THE MUSIC BUSINESS

Tony Hatch   90p

ARE YOU the next superstar? Is your son? Your grand-daughter? Your neighbour?

Fame and fortune are waiting for someone who is now stuck in a dead-end job dreaming of stardust.

Have *you* got what it takes? And if you have, do you know what to do about it?

Tony Hatch does.

He started as a tea boy in a music publisher's office. Today he is right at the top: a highly-paid composer, arranger and record producer with a string of hits under his belt.

Lately he has become even more famous for his perceptive straight-talking on TV's talent show, New Faces.

Now he has put everything he has learned in 15 successful years in showbusiness into one entertaining, revealing book.

Use the special order form at the end of this book.

Keep young and beautiful
with DAVID HAMILTON

EVERY WOMAN DREAMS of staying young and beautiful. But how?

When disc-jockey David Hamilton asked that question on his BBC radio show, thousands of women sent him their favourite beauty tips.

Now he has put the best of *your* hints into a bright, readable paperback for beauty-conscious women.

It tells you how to keep your face fresh and creamy, how to make your eyes sparkle, and how to make your toes the smartest in town.

There is down-to-earth advice on avoiding dandruff, saving lipstick, preventing spots and dealing with wrinkles.

It explains what you can do about bruises, stains, headaches and pregnancy stretch marks.

And top models Felicity Devonshire, Tammi Etherington, Linda Payne and Cherri Gilham have added their beauty secrets as a special bonus.

BEAUTY TIPS FOR WOMEN David Hamilton 40p

Use the special order form at the end of this book.

CROSSROADS

'I NAME THIS MOTEL CROSSROADS, AND GOD BLESS ALL WHO STAY HERE!'

So began the television phenomenon of the sixties and seventies. More than 7,000,000 homes tune in every time Crossroads is broadcast.

Malcolm Hulke is another success story. A member of the Crossroads scriptwriting team, and script editor of the serial for four years, he is also the author of several bestselling books.

Now he has created a heartwarming series of novels based on the Crossroads scripts.

REMEMBER the love affair between Meg's brother Andy Fraser and the widow Ruth Bailey?

REMEMBER how Sandy left school at 15 to make tea on the local paper – and grew up overnight?

REMEMBER when Jill Richardson fell in love with Philip Winter, the prisoner on the run?

For long-standing Crossroads fans the books bring back a flood of memories; and for recent converts they fill in the background to Meg's motel.

They also tell the stories the programme glossed over, and show the scenes television could not screen.

CROSSROADS – A NEW BEGINNING Malcolm Hulke
40p
'As entertaining as the programme itself' – *Daily Mirror*

CROSSROADS – A WARM BREEZE Malcolm Hulke
45p

Use the special order form at the end of this book.

THE BIG HIT Symon Myles 45p

IN THE third Apples Carstairs thriller, Apples and his two lovers encounter blackmail, corruption and murder in the world of pop music.

Also by Symon Myles:

THE BIG NEEDLE   45p
('Breathtaking pace' – E. News)

THE BIG BLACK   45p
('Unputdownable' – SE London & Kentish Mercury)

Use the special order form at the end of this book.

READ WELL WITH EVEREST

We hope you have enjoyed this book. If you have any difficulty in obtaining Everest publications, please fill in the form below and list the titles you require.

To:

Everest Books, Cash Sales Department, 4 Valentine Place, London E1.

I enclose purchase price plus 10p postage and packing per book by cheque, postal or money order. (No currency.)

NAME (*block letters*) ....

ADDRESS ....

....

....

While every effort is made to keep prices down, it is sometimes necessary to increase prices at short notice. Everest Books reserve the right to show new retail prices on covers which may differ from those previously advertised in the text or elsewhere.